PAGES

Pages

Innovative Bookmaking Techniques

Linda Fry Kenzle

krause publications

700 E. State Street • Iola, WI 54990-0001

krause
publications

700 E. State Street • Iola, WI 54990-0001

Photography by Nick Novelli.
Photo in album on page 72 by Nick Novelli.
Illustrations by Larry Meyer.
Cover background and template page background are of handmade cloth-covered books by the author.
Book Design by Jan Wojtech.

Acknowledgments
   Thanks to the many people who supported my effort in creating this book: Shirley Miller at Loew-Cornell, Inc., Gary Wolin of McManus & Morgan, Inc., Scott Rice at The Wisconsin Paper Council, and the folks at Daniel Smith, Mead Paper, American Blueprint, Aiko's, and the Paper Source. Also to the helpful reference librarians at the Internet Public Library, Fox River Grove Library, Barrington Area Library, and Crystal Lake Public Library.

   Thank you to all of the guest artists: Lina Atlake, Pat Balwin, Anne-Claude Cotty, Susan Kapuscinski Gaylord, Julie Harris, Susan Hensel, Charles Hobson, Mimi Labrucherie, Mary Ellen Long, Gail Looper, Patricia Malarcher, Beverly Nichols, Karen Page, Miriam Schaer, BarbaraSeidel, Anne Hicks Siberell, Joan Soppe, Mary Tyler, and Katherine Venturelli who generously shared their work shown in *Pages.*

   Thanks to Susan Keller and Mary Green who first supported the idea of this project. Thanks to Deborah Faupel, Barbara Case, Gabrielle Wyant-Perillo and everyone else at Krause Publications for bringing this book into print.

   Special thanks to Don Carlo and the rest of my family who made a huge additional effort during my broken ankle incident and the long recovery as I continued on this project. My love back to you.

Library of Congress Cataloging-in-Publication Data
   Fry Kenzle, Linda.
      Pages: Innovative Bookmaking Techniques / Linda Fry Kenzle
      p.128 cm.
      Includes index, bibliography, resources.
      ISBN 0-87341-547-7
         1. Bookmaking techniques. 2. Handmade paper. 3. Templates.
         I. Fry Kenzle, Linda. II. Title.
                                                         97-74245

To my charming son,
Joshua,

who is an artist in his own right.

Introduction

Books are powerful. Between the covers of a book lies a new world created by the author. It may be a journal of one's innermost thoughts, a sketchbook of an artist's drawings, a book of family recipes, a summer vacation scrapbook, schematics for a new invention, the musings of a future philosopher, a book of pressed flowers to preserve the memories of last years garden, or poems to a lover. The world of books is endless. You are the creator.

This book is an entree into that wonderful world of bookmaking. Even if you have never created a book before, here you will find interesting ways to express yourself. You can keep it simple and easy, or create a distinctive artful piece.

The presentation found here is built upon the classic book forms: the scroll, the folded book, the Japanese-style bound book, and the album. Also included is a portfolio that can be used as a slipcase for a book or can become a "book" containing loose pages.

Today, thanks to the many artists who have explored the book form, a book may not be only a traditional book of two covers containing pages. The boundaries to book making have been broken. Now books can indeed use the regular book form, but they can also be constructions. Artists like Mimi Labrucherie take pieces of cardboard, stack them, and cut them into circular shapes to evoke a statement about the disappearance of languages. Susan Kapuscinski Gaylord and Julie Harris find inspiration in nature's cast-offs to create books that look as if one would find them on the forest's floor just waiting to be discovered. Modern books may contain a message and the message isn't always concealed behind the covers of the book. Miriam Schaer's brilliant *No More Dishes to Wash* is an excellent example.

Throughout this book you will find a gallery showing the creations of an international group of artists working in the book arts.

Look into these private worlds, and be prepared to be amazed at the technique, the color and the form, that can be expressed in a book.

In the back of this book I offer a section called Potentials. Here you will find ways to make the book you create uniquely yours. The techniques cover a wide range of surface embellishments, and other methods to conjure up a unique presentation. Perhaps you'd also like to try your hand at making your own paper?

My love of the book started long ago. As a child I sketched colored charcoal drawings of birds for a "Flying" book, made annual Christmas wish books using cut-outs from catalogs, and wrote little crudely-illustrated story books which my mother sewed together on a sewing machine. As a teenage I wrote books of passionate poetry, and overly-dramatic stories illustrated in scented inks.

In 1973, my new husband, Don Carlo, and I purchased a mimeograph machine and each published a book: his was poetry, mine was crafts. I started designing "the doll as art" patterns that actually sold quite well. This was sheer indulgence as we both had jobs in other areas. By 1976 we jumped in with both feet and purchased a printing business. We named it Third Coast Printing & Art Press. Along with bill-paying accounts like Playboy, Hilton, and TSR Hobbies we published poetry, anthologies, broadsides, and New Wave comix by the likes of Gary Whitney and Scarlett Moon. We sold the going concern five years later. Since that time I have continued publishing - both self-publishing (sometimes in tiny handmade editions of 5 or 10 copies; others in 500 to 1000 lithographic copies), and in being published by large publishing companies. I simply love books...touching them, making them, reading them.

Indeed I hope you will venture into this land of handmade books. It is accessible to everyone from a seven year old child to a centenarian. Get creative. Sing your own song.

L.F.K.

Lake Geneva, Wisconsin

"Quickly…give me your hand" by Linda Fry Kenzle.
Triangle book, yellow watercolor paper, rubber stamped and painted, brass coils.

approaching the book
      as a handcrafted art object
      not only a place for text and image
      but as a sculptural object
      creating a playful and tactile
      interactive experience
                    ——barbara seidel

Contents

Part Four: Design Potentials

Part Five: Paper Enhancement Methods

Part Six: Artist Showcase

Part Seven: The Last Word

PART ONE
Book Basics

Photo by Author

"History of Writing" by Mimi Labrucherie Constructed of 300 sheets of posterboard stacked and cut in a spiral that forms 142 stairs and a tower. Each stair has an example of a historic and/or foreign alphabet. Inside the piece are 7 chambers that house further examples of writing: hiero-glyph on papyrus, cuneiform on clay, Australian message stick, quipu, found object with imaginary alphabet/writing, phaisdos disc, and a book with a verse in English, The book further has 4 pop-up human figures each with a foreign language on their backs and English on their fronts symbolizing that they are turning their backs on their native languages in favor of English.

A BRIEF HISTORY OF BOOKS

Two great inventions, the discovery of paper and of printing, did more than just about anything else, to further our modern communications.

Beyond the early clay tablets, where symbols were cut into the surface, the papyrus of the Middle East is considered the beginning of actual writing on a portable surface. The word "paper" is derived from "papyrus". Early Egyptians made papyrus sheets out of reeds from **Cyperus papyrus**. They cut the stalks, placed them at right angles to each other and pressed them into sheets. The papyrus was fashioned into scrolls and the writing was done in narrow columns with reed pens. Greeks made writing sheets out of vellum which was made of animal skins. Silk was used as a writing surface in the Far East.

Philiadelpia
1690 First Paper Mill
in America

Mayans
200 B.C. Invent
Codex Book

Modern paper takes its roots to China in A.D. 105. Ts' ai Lun, a court official, used mashed fibers to create paper. It is believed that he used the inner bark of mulberry, mixed with rag bits, hemp, and derelict fishing nets to make a stable paper. This is quite similar to the way handmade paper is created today.

Around A.D. 300 the codex made of sheets of vellum folded into a gathering evolved. This is the ancestor to the book you are holding in your hands right now.

By A.D. 610 Buddhist monks spread the art of papermaking to Japan. The Japanese embraced the new paper and to this day it is used without abandon.

War erupted between the Chinese and Arabs 150 years later. In an attempt to end the bloodshed the Chinese taught papermaking to the Arabs.

During the Crusades, papermaking spread to Europe. The first paper mill was established by the Arabs in Spain. From there it expanded throughout Europe with paper mills springing up in Italy, France, and Germany. For several hundred years, paper was made exclusively by hand. Books were hand-lettered, usually by monks. The beautiful **Book of Kells**, named for the Kells Monastery in Ireland, was created at this time.

Books were still for the privileged few. Huge books were paraded down the streets for everyone to ogle, by not to read. At this time they were still revered as religious artifacts, not books as we know them today.

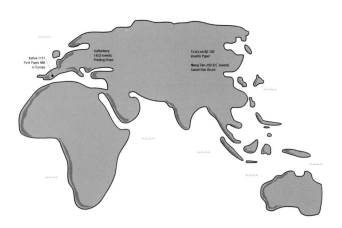

Xativa 1151
First Paper Mill
in Europe

Guttenberg
1453 Invents
Printing Press

Ts' ai Lun AD 105
Invents Paper

Meng Tien 250 B.C. Invents
Camel Hair Brush

The invention of a movable type printing press, by Johann Gutenberg in 1453, revolutionized the printed word. Books became objects of physical beauty. Illuminated letters began chapters and classic type faces were invented. The creation of magnificent religious books, called the **Books of Hours**, are considered by some to be the most exquisite books ever published.

During the1600s, enormous quantities of religious publications were purchased. The written word, the book, came into the hands of the people. Literacy increased, book production increased, and the world of publishing was born.

Frontispieces, illustrations done in engraving, began to appear in books. Caslon, Baskerville, and Bodoni created elegant typefaces. Books were ultimately readable and, at the same time, beautiful.

By 1750, machines entered the world of paper. A machine to break down pulp fibers was invented in Holland. In 1798, the continuous roll of paper was invented by Nicholas Louis Robert. Later this process was improved by the Fourdrinier brothers of England.

In 1840, the process of using logs for paper was invented by a German man named Friedrich Gottlob Keller. Rapidly, other scientists improved on Keller's process and brought paper into the disposable market we have today. "Dime novels" and inexpensive editions of the classics brought about huge scale production.

By the late 1800s, school children discarded their slates and entered school with bundles of paper under their arms, ready to start a new semester.

Today disposable papers made of tree pulp are consumed by the tons. We use paper every day - from a guest check at a cafe, to a to-do list, to those ubiquitous bills. The advent of the computer hasn't slowed down our need for paper. We still prefer a hard copy to reading on an eye-tiring screen. Our need to communicate by written means is high in a well-schooled, information hungry society. Consider the thousands of books published each year.

Zoom into the next century, and look back to the primal ways of papermaking and creating books. Find an elegance and an honest expression in the simple book forms. Challenge the boundaries and take the forms to a higher, artistic level. We, once again, will be intrigued by beautiful books in small editions.

Celebrate the book!

"Making a book, like reading a book, begins with a thrust of imagination..." – Patricia Malarcher

PARTS OF A TRADITIONAL BOOK

Before investigating the ways to create books, note what makes up a traditional book.

Familiarize yourself with the terms for the outside of a book:

The **cover**, front and back, is formed in one piece. It can be made of paper, cloth, leather, or other materials. It is designed to grab the potential readers attention. The back cover, on a commercially published book, is used as a romance piece. It encourages the reader to open the book and discover what's inside.

The **spine** is the area between the front and back cover. It serves to fasten together the pages, or signatures, of the book. The spine is important since, once placed on the shelf, it is the only part of the book posting the title, author and publisher.

A **signature** is a gathered stack of, usually 32, pages.

The inside pages should have a **margin** at all edges. A margin allows breathing room and creates an esthetically beautiful piece. The **gutter** is the point at which the pages of the book are united. Type is not readable if placed in the gutter. Many commercial designers place photo illustrations so they fall into the gutter. I personally find this annoying, especially in an instructional manual or art book. The reader is unable to clearly view what is being presented. In artistically-designed books this is a widespread and acceptable practice, but here I am speaking of traditional books.

Recto is the term for the right-hand page of a book. It always has an odd **folio**, or page number. **Verso** refers to the left-hand page, an even number.

The first page is the **half-title page**. It states only the title or name of the book. The second page is the **title page**. Here you will find the title, author's name, the publisher's name, and place of publication.

On the verso side of the title page is the **copyright page**. This includes notice of the author's copyright, usually stated Copyright, or ©, and year by authors name. All rights

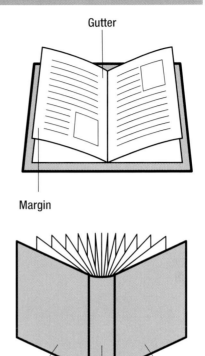

Gutter

Margin

Back Cover   Spine   Front Cover

Head

Tail

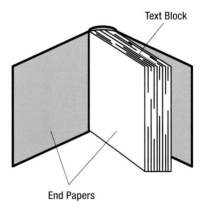

Text Block

End Papers

reserved and a line referring to the publishers name, place of publication, and zip code, fall on the lines just below the copyright notice.

"About the Linens" by Joan Soppe Letterpress, mixed media and handmade paper

Additional information can then be added:
- Editor, illustrator, and photographer credits.
- Country of manufacture.
- Library of Congress Cataloging-in-Publication Data. This refers to the way the book will be shelved in libraries, and contains the ISBN or International Standard Book Number. This important number is used by people who want to order the book. The numbers are available only to publishers and are assigned in groups. Specific publishers and book titles can be identified by these numbers.
- Categories for the book are given to allow librarians to properly shelve the book. The Decimal System Number and the Library of Congress numbers also are stated.
- Lastly, the edition of the book will be stated in a series of numbers.

The following page is usually the **table of contents**. This gives an overview of what can be found in the book, and is usually stated by section names and chapter titles.

The **preface** and/or **introduction** can be found next. The preface and introduction herald the new book and may be written by the author or a well-known personality. Usually an introduction is written by the author. This introduction provides an overview to the reader of what brought about the writing of the book. It will often discuss the contents of the book. If written by a personality, it is usually a complimentary salutation to the author and/or the subject. This may also be called a **foreword**.

The **acknowledgments** provide an opportunity for the author to thank others for their participation in the making of the book. This can be front matter, For many years, the acknowledgments has been placed as front matter. However, since this is information the author may not know until the book is nearly completed, and because books are now submitted on computer disks, it now is often found at the back of the book. Either is acceptable.

All of what has been discussed is called the **front matter** because it comes before the text.

The **text** is the meat of the book. It usually starts with chapter one and proceeds through all of the necessary chapters to create a thorough discussion of the main topic.

Photo by Oman Studios

Observe what constitutes the back matter:

The **appendix** usually contains graphs and other supplementary information not included in the text.

The list of works, used by the author as research in writing the book, is referred to as the **bibliography**. The size and depth of bibliographies often seem to be absent from books and appear to be falling out of favor. Authors rarely create a subject out of the air and I would love to see a revival in this area. The bibliography gives the reader a valuable resource to delve further into the subject.

Authors, well-known in their field, will sometimes title the bibliography **suggested reading** which implies that the texts were not used for research. The author is actually supplying a list of books he or she deems of value on the subject.

The listing of **resources** gives the reader mail-order sources for supplies. This list is especially appreciated by readers who are not in close proximity to a major metropolitan area, or in the case of any difficult to find items.

A good **index** serves as a reference guide to names, places and subjects included in a printed work. The index should be full and interesting. This is the back door into your book.

Conclusively, the publisher may add a **colophon**. This is a short statement giving facts pertaining to the books publication.

After the pages are printed and **collated**, or put together in the correct order, a cover is selected and bound into a book. At this point it is ready for presentation to the public.

Use these book basics with **The Handsome Bound Book** detailed in on page 51. Dig out that novel you wrote, write a family history loaded with anecdotes or gather together your poetry. Then publish on your computer. Gather together the pages of your

"Home on the Range" by Linda Fry Kenzle Album cover with spray painting, beading, photograph

Photo by Artist

book and bind it with a beautiful cover. Rather than a typically bound manuscript, you now will have created a real book. Give the book to family member, friend or agent. You are the author of your own life.

Creative Expression

With the knowledge of the basic traditional ways a book is created, I encourage you to feel free to break the rules. You may noticed how many times I use the word "usually" when discussing the creation of traditional books.

This is because everything in bookmaking is open to interpretation. Let your creativity run free and express yourself.

Travel with me and create simple book forms such as the scroll, the folded or accordion book, and the Japanese-stitched book. Explore the portfolio and the photo album. Learn techniques to make ordinary books extraordinary.

BOOK THEMES

Personal Journal - Use this book to express your feelings; record your personal journey.

Travel Log - Record data from a USA road trip or an European vacation.

Baby Book - Record babies first tooth, first word, first step.

School Days - Continue the baby book into the school year. List achievements and paste in yearly photographs.

Gardener's Journal - Keep track of what's happening in the garden.

The Great Novel - Everyone has a novel inside of them; write one.

Photo Album - Everyone loves pictures; save yours.

Wedding Remembrance - Record the names of those attending your wedding, what everyone wore, the music, the cake, the wedding colors.

Recipe Book - Write in precious family recipes and new ones of your own.

Birder's Journal - Connect with Mother Nature by keeping a bird list.

Book of Poetry - Write your own poetry or cite your favorite poets.

Sketchbooks - Always have a sketchbook handy to record impressions of the world around you.

Samplers - Do calligraphy or mount hand embroidered samples.

Day Books - Keep track of your daily activities.

Work Books - Keep track of hours worked and wages received.

Primers - Write a concise treatise on a single subject.

Woman's Book - Record yearly check-ups and personal information.

Gift Books - Make a unique gift for a friend.

Watercolor Sampler - Create small books to record small paintings.

Party Planner - Plan out a party theme, music, appetizers, etc.

Autograph Book - Collect autographs of those you admire.

Flower Press - Fill a book with onion skin paper and fresh flowers. Place under a heavy weight.

Anniversary Remembrance - Create a special book of old photos, remembrances, and the party you threw for the celebrants.

Scrapbook - Fill with anything you want to commemorate.

Funeral Book - Remember the deceased with a book honoring their life. Include photos and other remembrances.

Vacation Scrapbook - Did you spend a month at a dude ranch or a spa? Record it.

Photo by Artist

"Inside Secrets" by Anne Hicks Siberell

Clipper - Save published articles about a person or subject of personal interest.

Birthday Invitation - Use scrolls or folded books as unique invitations.

Scroll Maps - Draw a map to your hideaway cabin or fishing cottage.

Show Book - Do you sell on the craft show circuit, the antique circuit, or to art galleries? Record sales and experiences.

Collector's Book - Save pictures and articles pertaining to your collectibles.

Cartoon Book - Write and illustrate your own cartoons.

Wish Book - Use pictures and words to illuminate how you foresee your life in the future.

Moving Book - Leave a present for the future owner of your house. Tell them about the little particularities or where the perennials are planted. Or, use this to record all of the places you live during your lifetime. Include pictures.

Documentation Book - Record information about your paintings, sculpture or artist's books.

Almanac - Keep a written piece on the weather - full moon, when it rained and accumulation.

Design Book - Record personally appealing colors and textures. Use as a reference when planning your next decorating theme.

Sign all of the books or use a signature stamp as mentioned on page 85.

Number the books by editions. The first number designates the number of the specific book and the second number is the total number of copies in the edition. For example, a book numbered 3/10 is number 3 in an edition of 10 books.

I invite you to join me in a journey of hand bookmaking.

PART TWO

Write, Draw & Create

PAPER AND TOOLS

This chapter explores the paper possibilities when using charcoal sketches, watercolor washes or acrylics. Illustrated are various paper compositions which then progress to available media. Media possibilities include, but are not limited to, paint, pens, pencils, dyes and water-color.

There are three classifications for paper; machine-made, mold-made and handmade.

Machine-made paper covers most of the paper available. These papers are entirely machine made and usually contains a high-content of wood pulp. Many printers papers are made by machine.

Mold-made paper is produced on a machine where a vacuum pulls the pulp onto a screen. Most watercolor paper is created by this method.

ABOUT PAPERS

Handmade paper is composed by hand using a mold and deckle, as done centuries ago.

Papers are available in two categories; printers papers and art papers.

Printers papers are designed foremost for functionality. They can be printed on by a printing press. They can be written on with the usual media of pencils, ball point and felt tip pens. Papers can be made of any fiber from tree pulp to cotton rags. The higher the rag content, the more fine and expensive the paper. A paper with rag content will far outlast tree pulp. Newspaper, meant for one days use, begins almost immediately to break down.

The intended usage of the book, and the impression you wish to impart, will determine the type of paper you choose. Formal wedding invitations are done on exquisite rag paper to create an atmosphere of a celebration, a rite which one hopes will endure. An annual sales presentation is done on an elegant paper to give the impression of a strong, stable company. A booklet of poems by a teenager or a child's finger-painting may be done on a budget-priced, unprinted newsprint.

Journals and art pieces should be made of acid-free papers. These will last indefinitely, if properly stored at a correct temperature and in a moisture-free environment. Acid-free papers are marked acid-free, archival, or artists quality. They denote a pH reading of 7 which is neutral (neither acid or alkaline). Acid-free is designated all the way up to a reading of 9 pH. Acid, below 7 pH, is very destructive over time and will destroy the paper.

"I wrap fiber around Aspen trees to capture their strength and form; I bury paper under winter snows to document process and transition; I arrange indigenous elements into symbolic forms."

–Mary Ellen Long

WORKING WITH PAPER

" Album #8" by Lina Atlake Bead bound album adorned with Japanese papers and materials found in an estate sale sewing basket. Album is filled with black pastel drawing paper.

Working with paper is rather straight forward. Paper can be cut, torn, stretched and folded. Most paper has a grain, as does woven cloth. If a precise fold is desired, fold with the grain. If paper is folded against the grain, the paper will tear in an erratic manner and separate the fibers.

Educate yourself to paper grain. The influence of parallel fibers, the grain, is important when bending or tearing paper.

Take a piece of newspaper and tear it in one direction. Tear again in the other direction. The straight edge, follows the direction of the fiber and is *with* the grain. The more jagged edge was torn *across* the grain.

It is also possible to find the grain by holding one edge of the paper with the fingertips of both hands. Allow the paper to bend. If the paper bends gracefully, under it's own weight,

and has quite a bit of curve, it is *with* the grain.

Rotate the paper ninety degrees and hold the edge of the paper. Again, allow the paper to bend. If the paper curves less and is stiff, this is *across* the grain. It may take a bit of practice to feel the grain.

Two other ways to find the grain are as follows; cut a small piece of paper and fold it, first in one direction then in the other. The direction that folds smoothly is *with* the grain. Or, cut a small piece of paper and lay it in a shallow saucer of water. The paper will curl *with* the grain.

Paper manufacturers commonly state the grain as the second number in the size. For instance, a paper measuring 11" x 17" will have the grain along the 17" side. This is not always the case and it is best to use one of the previous tests if the grainline is important to your project.

Align the edges of the paper and create a sharp fold by finger pressing or using a bone folder. The bone folder is a flat bevel-edged tool used to press an edge. It is used by pressing against the paper edge and pulling towards the body.

Bypass the grain entirely and create a fold by scoring the paper with an Exacto™© knife. Intentionally fold against the grain to create a broken edge as in the piece *During* (color plate 97) . Be open to investigating the possibilities. ***Try. Test. Sample.***

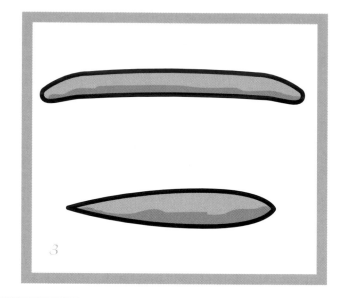

PRINTER'S PAPERS

Paper has a language of its own.
The following list will help decipher some of the paper terms:

• **Bond** is often used to do print-outs on your computer or typewriter. The flyers stuck under your wiper blades is bond paper! Bond is a thin and inexpensive type of paper.

• **Bristol** is a multi-ply sheet made of two sheets sealed together. Bristol is available in a soft, absorbent **vellum** finish or a hard, smooth **plate** finish.

• A **laid** paper refers to a texture created in the paper. Wires are laid relatively close on the mold during the papermaking process. This is usually a paper made with a high rag content and is considered a fine printing paper.

• **Linen** finish resembles linen cloth with a subtle horizontal and vertical wire pattern.

• **Pebble** finish creates a slightly bumpy surface.

• **Recycled** paper refers to any type of paper made of post consumer waste. It is boiled down and remanufactured.

Any of these papers can be put through your printer if the weight is correct. Be sure the **watermark** reads correctly. The watermark is an impression in the paper made by a wire shaped into a logo and embossed during the papermaking process. This mark denotes the correct side of the paper.

• All papers come in weights.

• **Cover weight** is heavy, and is used for covers.

• **Text weight** papers are lighter in weight and will feed through a printer. The weight of a paper is determined by the number of pounds in a ream. A ream is 500 sheets of paper of a standard size. The standard for bond is 17" x 22", text is 25" x 38", and cover is 20" x 26". For instance, a 90lb paper is a sheet from a ream of 22" x 30" (one paper size) that weights 90lbs. A thin onion skin paper weights only 9lbs, a drafting vellum runs 16lbs, text paper weighs around 20lbs, and a cover stock runs 60 to 120lbs.

Examine the types and weights of papers at your local office supply store or at your local print shop. The printer may give you some of their outdated paper sample books. Select the type of paper that will function best for the project you are undertaking.

ART PAPERS

While most printers papers are machine made, many art papers are handmade using centuries old techniques. Art papers cover both the artist's papers, such as Arches, that you would purchase as a support for water-color paintings, and the exotic papers, like rice paper, that come from Japan and other countries. The textures, finishes, and earthiness of these papers are varied and beautiful. Purchase a batch from the suppliers listed in the **Resources Guide** on page 122, and see the works they will inspire.

Most of the art papers do not have grain and can easily be manipulated to interesting effects.

Corrugate. Crumple. Pleat. Pucker. Snip. Rearrange.

"Sunflower Chili" by Don Carlo Kenzle Poetry book bound in mat boards with Japanese stitching by LFK

EXOTIC PAPERS

Papyrus is a historic paper. (For ease, it is referred to as paper. Technically it is not a true paper as it is made of layers of the pith of the papyrus plant, placed together at right angles and dried. Rather than made of an interlocked pulp.) Papyrus is suitable for painting, drawing, matting/framing and book covers. In ancient tombs, dating back to 3000 B.C., it has been found in perfect condition.

Most of the following papers are made of hemp, kozo, mitsumata or gampi fibers. These fibers may be combined with a pulp of wood, bamboo, or straw.

Thai unryu, available in both handmade

and machine-made versions, is made of long-stranded kozo fiber. This a strong yet thin paper. This paper is sometimes shot through with gold threads or has a brilliant marbled pattern. Unryu is a good choice for the portfolio project on page 66.

The **Thai naturals** are beautiful papers that incorporate pieces of natural plants and flowers. They are available in three different weights and can be used for any artful project.

Japanese inlaid papers sometimes include Japanese maple leaves, ginkgo leaves, ferns, and butterfly wings fused between thin papers. These papers are exquisitely beautiful and dearly priced.

Mulberry papers (kozo) are created from mulberry bark. Additions of other fibers create a unique paper. It is very textural with a soft deckle edge.

Japanese momi-gami is a soft paper that has been coated with konyuakuv solution to create a strong, water-resistant paper. These papers are machine made then wrinkled by hand to create a very textural surface. Sometimes imitation gold powders are mixed with paste and spread on the momi-gami to create a special effects paper.

Japanese ogura papers are more familiarly known as the lace papers. They are called **lace papers** because "falling water" is sprayed through a stencil onto the drying sheets to intentionally create holes or lace. This paper is made of manila hemp. The lace papers can be mounted on an opaque paper. This captures the effect of lace and creates a more substantial paper.

Another elegant paper is the **Indian silk paper**. It is handmade from cotton and silk, sized to a neutral pH, and has a weight of 100lbs. From India we also get the very textural paper called, by some suppliers, "Coral Reef". This paper is a 105lb, neutral pH, and can be used whenever a strong paper is required.

Nepalese lokta paper, also known as Dayshing, is available in solid color versions, in a paper shot through with brightly colored silk threads, and in another merged with ferns. Originally this strong paper was used for valuable documents such as deeds.

Bark papers are produced by the Otomi Indians in Mexico. This a variable paper with a primitive appeal. It is good for opaque paint work and bookbinding.

Banana paper is another variable paper. It is made from banana stalks and has a woodsy aroma. Its color is dependent on the intensity of the sun on the day the sheets were dried in the Philippines.. On sunny days the

Japanese papers.

bright sun bleaches the color out to a soft taupe. On cloudy days the paper dries dark **Banana skin** is a translucent version of this paper.

Not all of these papers are sized or are pH neutral. Ask before purchasing.

Many of these papers have a soft, uneven **deckle** edge as opposed to a sharp cut edge. If necessary or desired, create a deckle edge by one of two methods:

A. Fold the edge of the paper. Hold a ruler on the fold of the paper and tear from the top down, or

B. Fold the edge of the paper and wet the fold line with a small paintbrush loaded with water. Then use the ruler as a guide and tear, or

C. Try the new deckle edge rulers that have recently appeared on the market.

Exotic papers are available in many more versions than listed. For example, look for metallics, tone-on tone patterns, papers with distinctly oriental imagery and wispy checkerboard-patterned rice papers. If visiting Chicago, plan to visit Aiko's and the Paper Source. You will be amazed at the variety of available papers. Both of these companies have sample books that can be mail ordered.

See the Potentials chapter on page 78 for instructions on creating your own paper. Instructions include all of the necessary instructions for turning pulp into beautiful sheets of handmade paper.

TRADITIONAL ART PAPERS

French-made watercolor papers by Arches™, Canson™, Rives™, Italian-made Fabriano™, and the English Waterford© papers from T.H. Saunders™ are some of the well-known brands in the traditional art paper category. Art supply stores carry many other brands as well. Primarily the watercolor papers are available in a soft, pristine white, but other, more difficult to find, pastels do exist.

Watercolor paper is available in 90lb, 140lb, 260lb, 300lb, and 400lb. The lower the number, the lighter the weight. The 260lb, 300lb and 400lb paper is board-like and works well as a cover. The 90lb and 140lb are good for pages.

Watercolor paper is available in three finishes; **cold-pressed**, **hot-pressed**, and **rough**.

Cold-pressed is the most widely used. It has a slight **tooth** or texture which watercolorist like because it holds onto the paint.

Hot-pressed is a very smooth, slick paper. It is difficult to control watercolor on this surface, but it works fine for drawing pens.

The paper classified as rough is self-definitive and the surface is gritty and textural.

All of these papers are sized and made of 100% cotton fiber with a neutral pH. If using water media, the lightweight versions need to be stretched. If these are not stretched, buckling and rippling will result and paint may travel into undesired areas.

To **stretch** the paper, dip it in a full tub of tepid water. Remove the sheet by one of the corners and let it drip to remove the bulk of the excess water. Use masking tape or staple the sheet to a hardwood art board. Take care to smooth the paper. After the large sheet has dried, cut it into pages. Mount the pages on small individual boards for field work.

Another idea is to cut 140lb watercolor paper into smaller pages and add two covers. At a print shop, have the pages bound with a spiral binding. This is an easy way to create painting journals to preferred size.

Et Cetera

Other art papers include **velour paper** - a fuzzy textured paper used for pastels and charcoal. Claybord™ has a coated surface for pencils, pens, acrylic, gouache, and even oil paint applications. Check out your local art supply store for other available types of supports. Examine the paper and feel the surface. Select papers that appeal to your senses.

Search. Test. Study.

TOOLS

"Our House, 1983" by Linda Fry Kenzle Two-way flip album

Photo by Artist

Tools are a key factor in producing exquisite books. The best tools, as in any fine craftwork, give immediate outstanding results. Avoid re-cutting or making other adjustments by purchasing good tools. With proper care, tools can last a lifetime.

Essential List of Tools:

T-square and drawing board - A metal T-square may cost a bit more, than the plastic or wood versions, but it will far outlast the others. Most importantly, it gives a much more accurate alignment across the length of the paper.

Select a hardwood drawing board with a true ninety degree edge.

With these two tools, a professional-looking piece can be produced.

Ruler - Purchase a metal 12" ruler divided into 16ths, and readable in either direction. The ruler is a handy tool for short cuts which

have already been marked on the paper. Again, the metal version is far superior; the cutter blade lies right up against the edge of the ruler, giving a more accurate cut.

Cutters - For years I have used, with great results, utility knives, such as Exacto™ brand and carpet knives. These knives cut accurate corners and small window cut-outs. My newest favorite cutting tool is the rotary cutter. I prefer the larger size to the smaller version as I seem to get better pressure. Don't use a scissors for cutting the papers; the cut will be off, even if you are following a marked line. Reserve the scissors for snipping corners, clipping off thread ends and for cutting cords.

A tabletop cutter is available in two versions and is handy for cutting stacks of text paper. The older style has a long-bladed handle on the side of the table that is brought down manually to cut. To prevent cutter marks from appearing on the papers, always cover the paper, to be cut, with an extra sheet of paper or a piece of thin chipboard. Occasionally sharpen the cutter blade. Call your local printer for a source or send it out to be sharpened and oiled. Be sure the blade is reinstalled in the proper position.

The second, modern-style tabletop cutter has a rotary cutter that travels along a metal strip. When the cutter blade becomes dull, it is replaced with a new one.

Tabletop cutters cut a relatively small number of sheets of paper at one time. Paper can be cut in small batches, or ask your local printer cut it for you. Ask the price. Some printers ask a minimum charge. Occasionally, the project may not warrant the cutting price. Printers prices tend to vary drastically. Appreciate a printer that will do your jobs at fair prices. This is a valuable relationship. Gift him/her with a handmade book!

Cutting mat - A self-healing mat is a wonderful surface on which to cut. Cuts disappear and don't create a ridge to disrupt the line you are presently cutting. Buy the largest size you can afford.

Awls, paper punches, and other hole-makers - I use a handcrafted, antique, bone-handled awl for any small jobs that require puncturing only a few sheets of paper. For larger jobs I use a scratch awl. This handy tool is available at hardware stores. The true use is to scratch measurement marks in wood and metal building materials. To use the awls, it is necessary to have a small rubber mallet and a board to protect the work surface.

Small-holed paper punches produce small holes that typically filled with the binding cord so they aren't apparent. Large-holed paper punches are filled with a smaller cord to give a naive look to finished pieces. This may be just the effect you desire; don't dismiss this as being too simple. Stay open-minded.

Professional printers use a drill press to create holes. The drill supports a variety of various-sized bits. It is possible to purchase a drill press, if you are doing a lot of punching, or take pages to the printer and request they drill holes on your measured marks.

Photo by Jeff Sabo

"Druid Diary" by Julie Harris Sticks and handmade paper

ANOTHER IDEA

Printers have a tool called a stitcher. This tool uses wire cut to different staple lengths, and can be used as an alternative way to bind books. The printed, folded, and collated books are opened up and stapled so that the ends of the staple fall in the center of the book. Books bound in this manner are called saddle-stitched. You can purchase a deep-throated stapler at an office supply for studio work that will handle most small booklets. I've used this, with great success, for two garden titles, Scented Geraniums: Enchanted Plants for Today's Garden, and Vines For

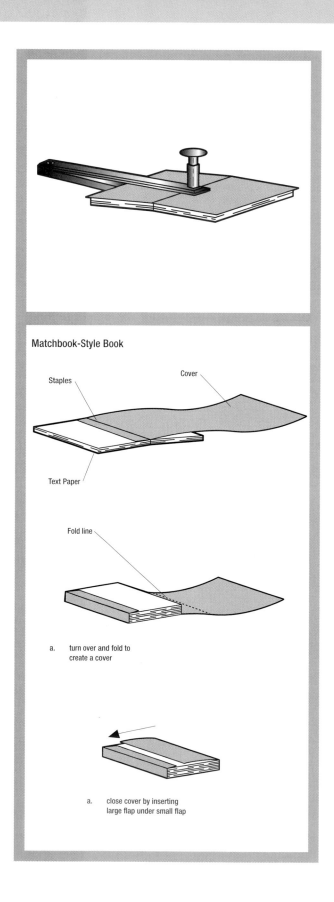

Matchbook-Style Book

Staples

Cover

Text Paper

Fold line

a.   turn over and fold to
     create a cover

a.   close cover by inserting
     large flap under small flap

America. Both editions sold out. This is a great way to distribute information to a wide audience at a reasonable cost for the designer, the publisher, and the purchaser. It is also good for poetry, or a monograph on any subject.

Adhesives

Selecting the adhesives you wish to use is a personal choice. Some artists prefer a reversible adherent like **wheat paste**, available in a cooked bookbinder's version. In the uncooked version, wheat paste is also called wheat wallpaper paste. It is mixed with distilled water, then allowed to sit for several minutes to thicken. The consistency can be adjusted with more wheat starch or distilled water. It will stay usable for one days work. The cooked version is preferred to the wallpaper paste due to the difference in consistency, but either work fine.

Flour paste is the type used by children in art class. It is made of flour mixed to a spreadable consistency with water. **Cornstarch** can be added to this mixture or used as a simple mixture with water.

Alum, available in the spice section of your local supermarket, is frequently added to the

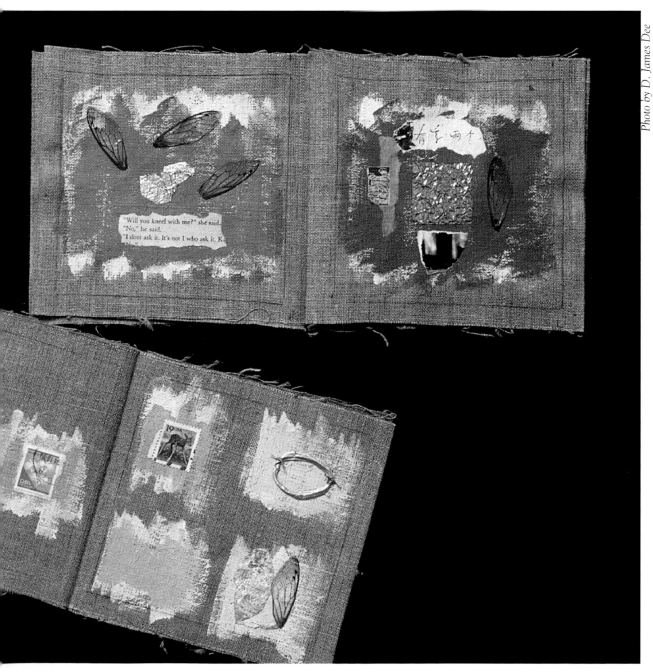

Photo by D. James Dee

"Field Journals: August" by Patricia Malarcher Linen, gesso, paint, found materials

paste mixtures. Oil of cloves and other essential oils such as lavender, bergamot, and rosemary can be added sparingly (a few drops to a quart) to act as a preservative and offer some protection from insect damage. Be sure to use an *essential* oil, which is the actual essence of the plant, as this does not stain paper. Any oil that does not specify the word *essential* is a fragrance oil made of essential oil added to a carrier oil, such as almond oil or vegetable oil. The fragrance oils will stain the paper and do not give the same benefits as the essential oils.

YES paste is a premixed wheat and glycerin paste. It can be used straight from the jar or thinned with distilled water.

PVA, polyvinyl acetate, includes the white glues such as Elmer's™ glue, Aleene's Tacky Glue™, and Lineco Neutral™ (neutral pH). They are premixed and ready to use. I especially like the Aleene's ™ Tacky glues for attaching bulky elements, to a collage piece, in a secure fashion.

Many book makers create their own paste recipes by combining PVA with any of the various powdered pastes. Pastes can also be used for decorative effects in creating paste papers. Mix three ounces wheat flour with one pint water; add any water-based paint for color, and pour the paste onto a sheet of paper. Manipulate, experiment and formulate.

If you wish to make sculptural pieces, experiment with applying **acrylic gel**, or adding a substrate for reinforcement.

Two newer adhesives include **Paper Cement** and **Zig 2-way** glue. Paper cement is formulated to prevent wrinkling, curling and shrinking. Zig 2-way glue is acid free. The Zig 2-way glue, when used wet (blue) makes a permanent bond, or can be used dry (clear) to form a tacky, temporary bond.

For children's work a **glue stick** may be preferable. The bond is good and clean-up is a cinch. No fuss, no muss.

Another option is to use the **spray adhesives** like Krylon®. One artist I know has used this adhesive very successfully with cloth covered books. The spray adhesives are easy to use but can present a health hazard. Spray in a well-ventilated area and wear a face mask.

Rubber cement is not recommended for book work, but is the right adhesive for attaching leather to leather.

Apply any of the adhesives with a wide flat paintbrush. Start in the center of the page and work outward. This will control the paper as it is moistened and assure a good seal on the books surface.

I also recommend **fusible web**. This product is found in sewing stores. Paper or cloth is ironed onto the webbing. The backing sheet is then removed and the paper/cloth is fused into place with an iron. The fusible web seal is excellent.

Find the adhesives that work best for you by testing and experiencing all of the various available adhesives. Sewing stores have many other adherents that work as well on paper as they do with cloth. Adherents choice will depend on the type of project being created.

"These [books] have been a great deal of fun, exercises in design and engineering, using high color with past papers."
—Anne-Claude Cotty

MAKING MARKS

When designing a handmade book, take into consideration the specific media that will be used.

For example:

Use lead pencils or ball point pens on bond or text papers.

If using colored pencils for quick sketches, use a bond or text. For colored pencils used with water, and built up in layers, a stronger paper is necessary, such as a 140lb watercolor paper.

Pen and ink pops on bristol plate paper. Although for special effects you may choose a cold-pressed paper.

Charcoal and pastels can be used on velour papers, cold-pressed or rough watercolor papers. After drawing on the page, spray with fixative and let dry. For added protection, cover the page with a loose cover sheet of onion skin paper.

Watercolors work best on watercolor paper. A cold-pressed 90lb weight is versatile for most types of work. If your style is to gouge the paper surface, use a heavier weight .

Inks and dyes need a thick paper such as a 140lb watercolor paper. Choose a heavier weight paper if you tend to drench the paper with the inks and dyes.

Acrylics, if worked thin, can use a watercolor paper ground. If you work in impasto, it would be better to use a canvas board, then insert the paintings in a portfolio. In my opinion, this is a great way to collect small oil paintings.

One small caveat: If you have selected a thin paper for a penetrating medium, such as markers, place a sheet of resistant paper under the page to prevent seepage. Do this to avoid ruining other beautiful work in your book.

As with all aspects of creative expression, anything goes, These ideas are just that: ideas.

Direct. Lead. Find your own way.

GET CREATIVE

Sample the creative world, and become impassioned to the many different ways of self expression, by walking into any well-stocked art supply store. Study the varieties of media and papers. Pick up any available brochures. Ask questions. Sign up for a class. Purchase a few colored pencils, some acrylic paint, a couple of tubes of watercolor (if you've only used pan paints, this is a treat), buy some different papers, adhesives, paint brushes, a painting medium, and anything else that catches your eye. Go directly home and play! Experiment with the possibilities of your purchased media.

Analyze. Examine. Probe. Explore.

Brush Shapes and Their Uses

The names for same or similar shapes, in various hairs or handle lengths, appear in parenthesis.
Unless noted by an *, these brush shapes are all included in our renowned La Corneille® Golden Taklon brush line.

Round - Use on point, or apply pressure to make thick-to-thin strokes.

Spotter - For fine detailing.

Liner - Continuous curved or straight lines. Vary thickness with pressure changes.

Ultra Round - Use as a liner on point. Full belly provides a reservoir for paint.

Jackie's Liner - Mid-length liner.

Script Liner (Long Liner) - Scroll work, flowing thick-to-thin lines. Length of hair holds more paint than a regular liner.

Shader (Flat) - Blocking in color, shading, blending, highlighting, and stroke work.

Chisel Blender (Bright) - Short, flat strokes and blending, especially useful with heavy mediums.

Angular Shader (Angle Flat) - Tight shading, curved strokes. Popular rose petal brush.

Wash (Wash/Glaze) - Washes, basecoating and applying finishes.

One Stroke (Stroke) - Long, flat lettering brush.

Filbert (Oval) - Strokes with soft edges. Blending. A natural flower petal shape.

Deerfoot Stippler - Texturizing brush. Use a dry brush and light, pouncing technique for fur, shrubbery, and soft backgrounds. '

Fan - Use dry or with tips loaded to create texture or smooth other brush strokes.

Rake® - Flat, texturizing brush with a naturally-fingered shape. Use for hair, grass, wood grain, feathers, and fur. **Filbert Rake**® creates the same effect with softer edges.

Dagger Striper - Long chisel edge for easy, fine lines. Vary pressure for thick-to-thin ribbon effect.

Miracle-Wedge® - Can be easily loaded with 3 different colors for a variety of stroke effects.

***Stencil** - Use a dry brush with very little paint and circular or stippling technique.

***Mop** - Blending and softening. Washes.

***Fabric** (Scrubbers) - Flats and tapered rounds. These brushes are sturdy enough to withstand a scrubbing or stenciling technique on fabric and other surfaces.

PERSONAL FAVORITES

Let me share with you some of my favorite materials currently residing in my on-the-go backpack/art bag:

Pencils: Stabilo Micro Graphites™ 2Uset 9H to 8B.

Colored pencils: Berol® Prismacolor™ 120 pencil set - good for wet and dry work.

Markers: Fine line Sharpies™, Pigma© Micron pens.

Drawing pens: Grumbacher™ artist pens in three sizes: 25mm, 35 mm, and 50 mm. Koh-i-noor™, Rotring Rapidoliners™, Rapidographs™.

Inks and dyes: Winsor & Newton™ inks, Jacquard™ dyes.

Watercolor: Winsor & Newton™ Cotman field box - it has everything necessary - paints, water flask, and a good quality brush.

Acrylics: Dick Blick™, Galleria™, and Liquitex™ in primary colors, black and white. Black and white allow mixing of any desired color.

Brushes: Winsor & Newton™, Daniel Smith™, Loew-Cornell™ in both flats and rounds of varying sizes.

Here is a handy chart compliments of Loew-Cornell™ that will help you choose the right brush:

Finally, I have a selection of papers, wipe cloths, a disposable palette, and a hand-bound journal stuffed in my bag. Fill your bag with personally seducing art supplies.

Don't purchase student quality supplies. This quality will not allow you to savor the beauty and ease of application, as will a high quality product. Even if you are just beginning, invest in excellent quality supplies.

Splurge. Experience the best.

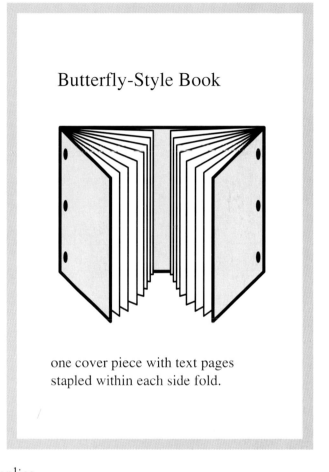

Butterfly-Style Book

one cover piece with text pages stapled within each side fold.

"...some books are done just for the joy of playing with different materials." —Gail Looper

PART THREE
Book Forms

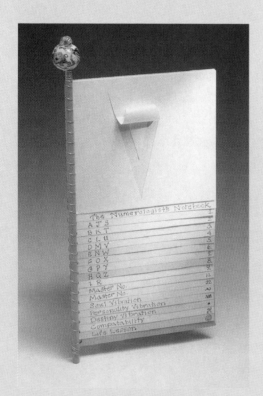

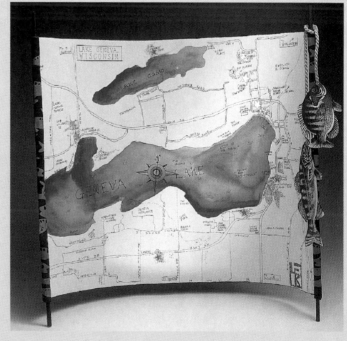

"Going Home" by Linda Fry Kenzle Scroll made of watercolor paper with ink drawing, fused to cloth, photocopied fish on heavy communion cord

THE VERSATILE SCROLL

The simplicity of this earliest of book form has a sensuous, moving quality. Occasionally it is called the rolled book. It can become anything. Dress it up or dress it down; either way it works!

MATERIALS

Paper: medium to heavy weight to support the dowels
2 dowels - any size
Adhesive

CONSTRUCTION

1. Cut paper to desired size. Paint, letter or further mark the paper as desired. That way anything you add will reach all of the way under the edges of the scroll.
Caveat: Don't put any essential details at the ends of the paper or they will disappear when the scrolls are added. Let dry.

2. Cut the dowels to the length desired. They should reach beyond the width of the paper. How much dowel exposed is a personal design decision. At this point, if desired, paint or stain the dowels. Let dry before proceeding.

3. Glue the dowels to the ends of the paper. Let dry thoroughly.

4. Around the dowel, finger press the edge of the paper. Roll the dowel and paper until the paper meets itself. This rolling procedure conditions the paper, making the next step is easier.

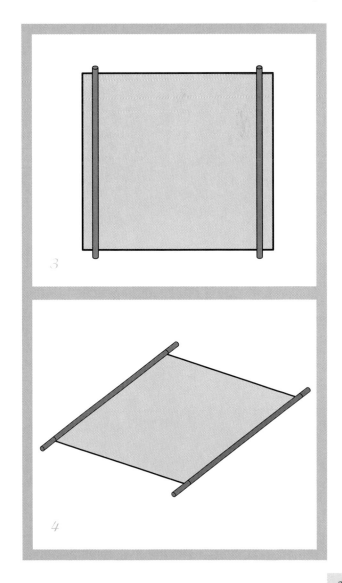

5. Place adhesive on the paper inside the rolled section. Roll until the paper meets itself. If you roll a bit further, the finished scroll will have a more professional finish.

6. To finish the other side of the scroll repeat from step 3.

7. Add weights to hold the dowels in place while they dry.

8. Add any further adornments to the dowels or scrolls.

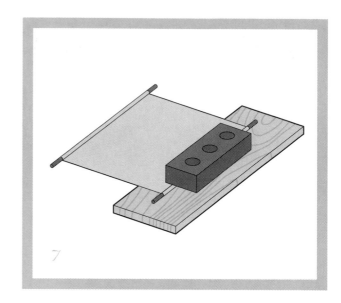

Considerations

• The paper selection should be of enough weight to support that of the dowels.

• Thinner papers can be built up to a substantial weight by layering them together.

• The scroll shown is a display piece and does not need to be unrolled any further than to show the map. A scroll can be any length and/or as long as the largest roll of paper you can locate.

• The dowel supports can be of any length and width. More likely the paper will determine the length of the necessary support.

• Alternative supports may be heavy cardboard tubes, Plexiglas™ rods, metal pipe, closet bars, or dowels made of potter's or polymer clay.

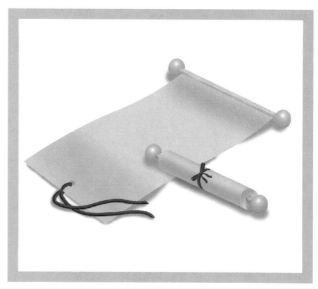

• To make a closed scroll attach cord or ribbon to one end and roll up the scroll like a paintbrush holder.

Ideas

- A scroll is a perfect book form for anything that needs to be recorded in an ongoing manner. For example, a genealogy chart.

- Small scrolls made of heavy raw silk make beautiful invitations to a dinner party.

- Done in bright colors, with peppermint sticks dowels, make a nice child's birthday party invitations.

- Map scrolls hark from ancient times. Now is a good time for a revival. Make scrolls using state maps, geological maps, land plats or the survey of your property.

To adorn the illustrated piece, I used color copier fish fused to a cloth backing with fusible web (instructions on manufacturer package). Other embellishment possibilities include tassels, large beads, or found objects.

"...art is one of the sanest, most healing, soul-healthy activities life has to offer."
——Susan Hensel

THE FINE FOLDED BOOK

The fine folded book is a sophisticated book form. It is occasionally referred to as an accordion book, and is very pure and elegant. Choose an exquisite paper and press it into evenly spaced folds. The value of this book lies in what is put on the paper - paint it, collage it, make drawings, or seek other unique presentations. A number of different folded book techniques are presented. Select the traditional accordion fold that is displayed in an expanded position or try the turtle wrap that creates a folded book with a spine.

"Juicy" by Linda Fry Kenzle Accordion book of watercolor paper with acrylic painting, deer fencing "Somewhere or There" by Linda Fry Kenzle Turtle wrap accordion book

FOLDED BOOK #1 - (TRADITIONAL)

MATERIALS

Cover stock
Cutter
Ruler
Pencil

CONSTRUCTION

1. Measure and cut a long rectangle of paper. Choose desired measurement.

2. Fold the sheet of paper in half.

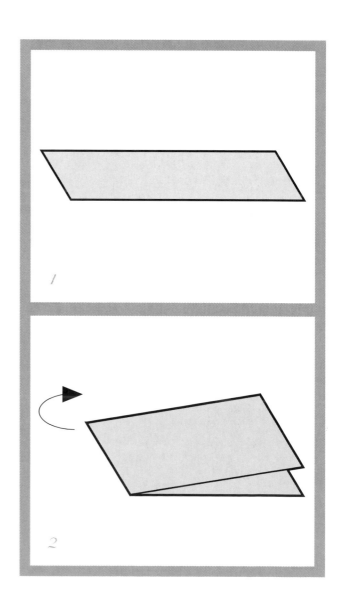

3. Fold one end halfway back.

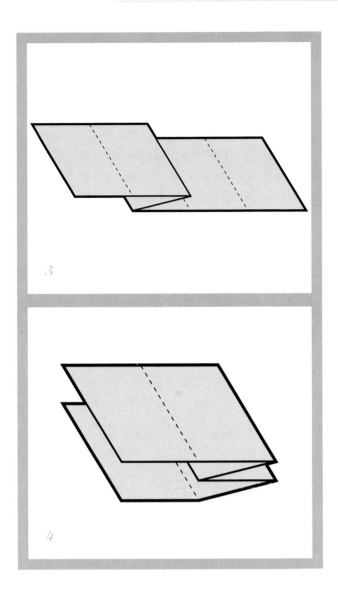

3

4

4. Turn the paper over and repeat on the other side.

5

6

5. Fold back the paper to create another page.

6 Repeat on the other side. This will result in a small folded book. A long sheet of paper is required to avoid the pages of the book becoming too narrow. Or, see considerations below for instructions on splicing strips of paper together.

7. Ornament book.

Considerations

First, determine the page size, then accordion fold, first front and then back, the paper. Cut off any excess paper at the end of the accordion. True up the top and bottom of the book with a rotary cutter, if necessary.

• To splice together the sheets:

A. Cut one of the two strips of paper you wish to join with a tab of 1/4" to 1/2". Glue the tab to the second strip or,

B. use a decorative join of a contrasting paper, ribbon, stitching, metal rings, etc., or

C. glue together two whole pages. By doing so, you will have a center page that is twice as thick as the other pages. View this as a design problem or enjoy the intentionally of it!

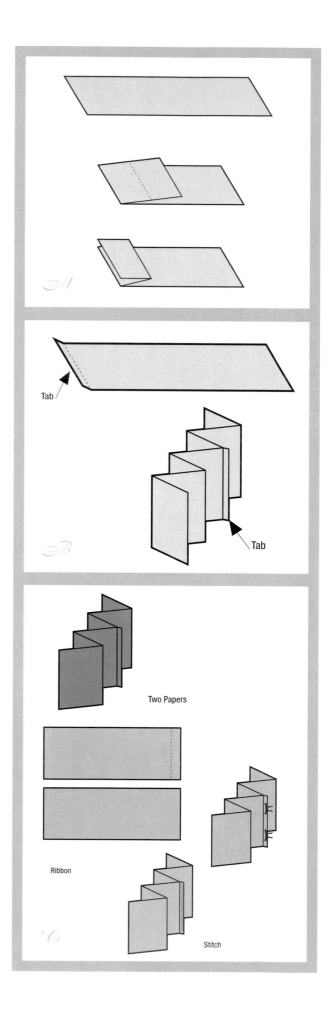

Ideas

Cut the top edge of the folded book into an uneven edge.

Create pop-ups between the pages.

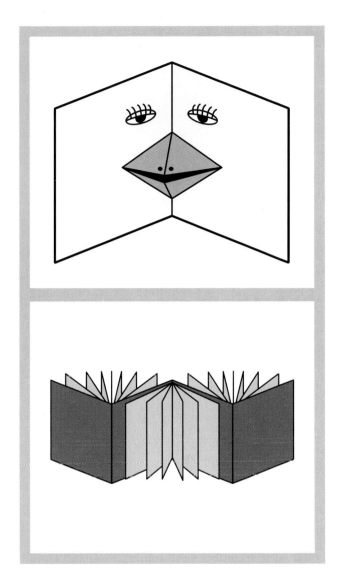

Fill the sections with signatures of folded printers papers and stitch them in place.

Bind each folded section with twine, ribbons, or wire. (See the "Alchemist's Blackboard" (page 86) in the Potentials chapter.)

Make a cover for this book:

1. Cut two pieces of cover stock the same size as the covers of the folded book.

2. Cut two pieces of decorative paper or cloth slightly larger (1/4") than the covers.

3. Glue the paper or cloth to the cover piece. Turn the raw edges to the back and glue to hold.

Repeat for the other cover.

4. Glue the covers in place on the folded book.

Book Cover #2: Adhere a piece of papyrus or other interesting material to the cover pages of the folded book.

FOLDED BOOK #2 - (TURTLE WRAP)

MATERIALS

Cover stock
Decorative paper (90lb or less)
Cutter
Ruler
Pencil
Adhesive

CONSTRUCTION

1. Construct the folded book following steps 1 through 6. Make sure that the "covers" of this book face in the same direction.

2. Measure one of the "covers". Measure and mark four templates on a piece of decorative paper. Depending on the size of the book, add a fold allowance of 1/4" to 1". Note that a larger book needs a larger fold.

3. Cut a spine cover of decorative paper to the same size as the "cover" and wide enough to cover the side of the folded book when it is held closed. In this case about 1 1/4" is appropriate.

4. Fold the tabs on the decorative to the backside.

5. Place the top tab of piece C into the top of piece B. The right side of each piece is to face outward.

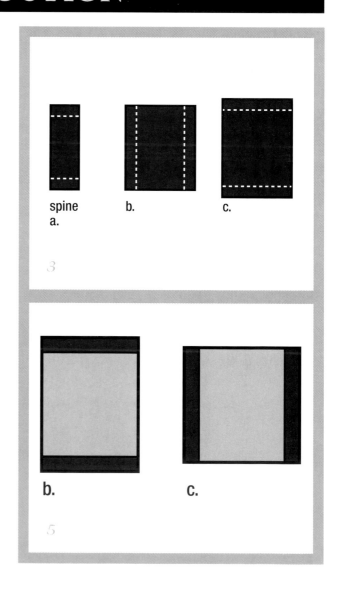

spine
a.

b.

c.

3

b.

c.

5

6. Bring down piece C and insert the other tab into the bottom of piece B. Both turtle wraps are to be flush.

7. Insert the "cover" in between the folded turtle wraps.

8. Repeat steps 4 through 7 for the other folded book "cover".

9. Insert the sides of the spine cover, in place, between the turtle wraps.

10. Leave the spine cover as is or glue it in place.

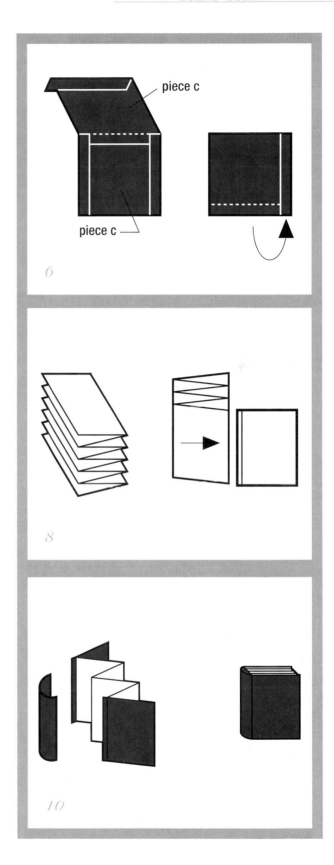

47

FOLDED BOOK # 3

MATERIALS

Cover stock (for folded book)
Decorative cover stock (for cover)
Cutter
Ruler
Pencil

CONSTRUCTION

1. Follow steps 1 through 6 of the Folded Book #1.

2. Place the folded book open on a piece of decorative cover stock. Trace and add a fold allowance to the sides, not to the top or bottom.

3. Cut out the decorative cover.

4. Glue the decorative cover to the open folded book. Fold over allowance and glue in place.

Options

Glue and end paper on the inside of each cover.
Glue on a spine over the cover for a finishing detail.

Ideas

Create a Flutter book by using a one-piece cover:

1. Open the folded book so the ends lie flat on a piece of paper and trace.

This is the cover template.

2. Adding an allowance of 1" around the template, cut out a cover from decorative paper.

3. Glue the folded book ends to the wrong side of the decorative cover. Make sure it is centered in place.

4. Clip corners. Fold and glue decorative cover in place on the inside covers of the folded book.

5. Cut and paste end papers in place over the books inside covers.

• Create a carousel book: Cut two slits in the covers of the folded book. Insert a dowel, stick or piece of wire.

• Create a Triangle book:

1. Cut a septagon of watercolor paper. Paint and decorate.

2. Measure into even triangle shapes. Cut, as shown. Fold back and forth into triangle shapes.

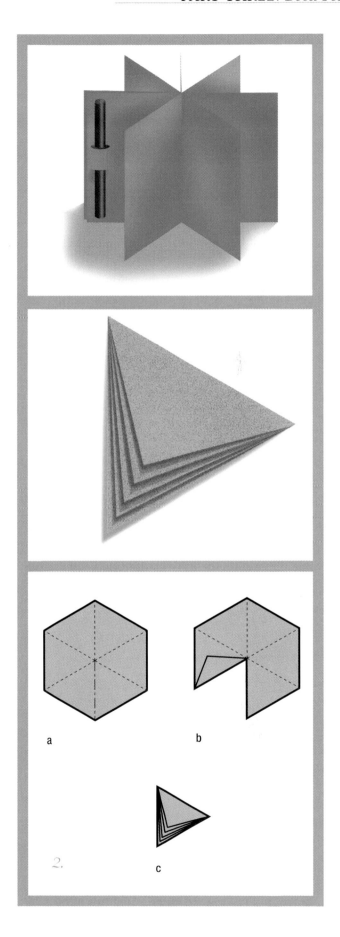

a

b

2.

c

- Make Outline books:

  Cut the folded books into shapes. Be sure to add a tab or connecting point so the shape stays connected. This is analogous to the paper snowflakes kids make for the Christmas tree.

"I work intuitively, beginning with a branch, an image, or a piece of folded paper and letting the book evolve naturally into an organic whole."
——Susan Kapuscinski Gaylord

THE BEAUTIFUL BOUND BOOK

"Spirit Journey" by Linda Fry Kenzle Bound book with flap cover, painted with silk dyes, waxed linen binding, velcro closure

THE BEAUTIFUL BOUND BOOK

This book form uses single sheets of unfolded paper cut to any chosen size. Create miniature books to huge tomes. Any number of pages can be accommodated from a thin chap-book of poems to a thick journal covering all 365 days of the year. The possibilities are endless. The last design decision is how to bind the book. Experiment with the binding configurations based on Japanese-stitched books that are illustrated at the end of this chapter.

MATERIALS

Interior paper
Scratch awl (available at hardware stores)
Small mallet
Ruler
Pencil
Cover paper
Waxed linen cord
Needle for bookbinding

CONSTRUCTION

1. Select and, if necessary, cut sheets of paper to the size desired. For the book shown, I used precut sheets of 60lb bond.

2. Measure and mark the side of paper for the binding. Use at least a 1/2" space between the hole and the spine edge of the proposed book.
Use the awl and mallet to create the holes in about twenty sheets of paper at a time.

You can also take the sheets to a printer or copy shop and have them drilled. Again, call around for prices as they will fluctuate greatly. Some shops will have an expensive minimum fee, others will drill the paper for a "song."

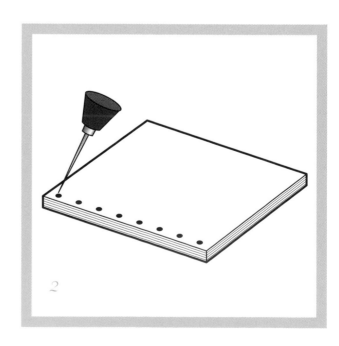

2

3. Measure the width and density of the paper:

In this example the back is 8 1/2", the spine is 1", and the front is 8 1/2", for a total measurement of 18".
Then measure the length, here it is 11".
Add an additional 4 1/2" if adding a flap 22 1/2" x 11".
These measurements will give the cover measurement of 18" x 11".

4. Select a cover stock and cut it to this measurement. Measure and score the wrap-around cover stock to accommodate the pages

Here's how:
5. To bind the pages to the cover, insert the stack of paper with the punched holes toward the spine into the cover. Be sure all pages are flush. Remove the top sheet of paper and lay it exactly square upon the cover. Punch holes in the cover. Turn the stacked "book" over and repeat this procedure on the back of the cover.

6. Cut a 4' length of waxed linen. Thread it onto a large-eyed needle. Begin by inserting the needle into the first bottom hole. Follow this pattern:

  Tie off.
7. Fold cover flap in place. Bevel flap. Attach Velcro closure.

When creating a theme book such as a Birder's Journal, a Birthday Bash, a Travel Log, a Guest Book, a Garden Journal, a Personal Journal or a Anniversary Salute, please see the template section of this chapter. The templates can be copied or scanned right out of the book or, use them as reference sheets to create personal computer-generated pages.

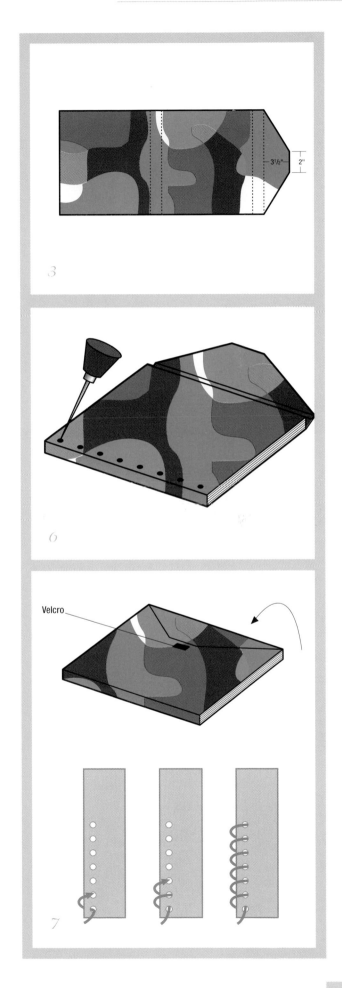

Considerations

Do surface decorations, such as spraying, marbling or sewing, to the cover before binding. Collage and any other enhancements can be added after the book is bound.

If you have uneven edges on the bound book do not try to even them up by cutting with a scissors. It will not be even. Take the book to a print shop and have them cut it with a professional cutter. Note: if the binding thread goes around the bead and tail you cannot trim these edges. Trim only the front edge.

Trim handmade books, with few pages, by using a steel ruler and a rotary cutter. Be sure to hold the ruler tightly in place.

BINDING PATTERNS

Select from any of the following binding patterns. Consider using binding materials such as ribbons, twine, heavy metallic threads, wire, beads on tiger tail, leather thongs, chain or strands of colorful telephone wire.

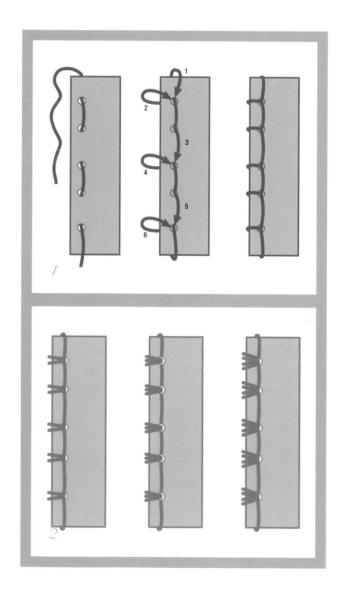

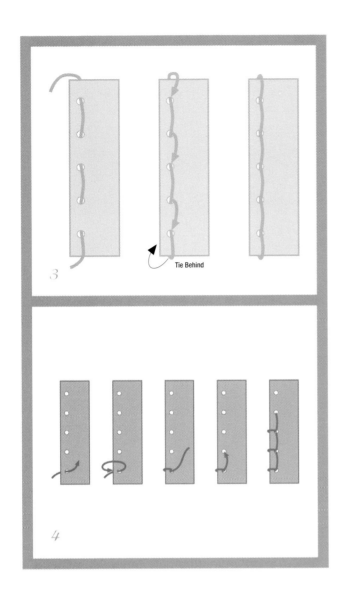

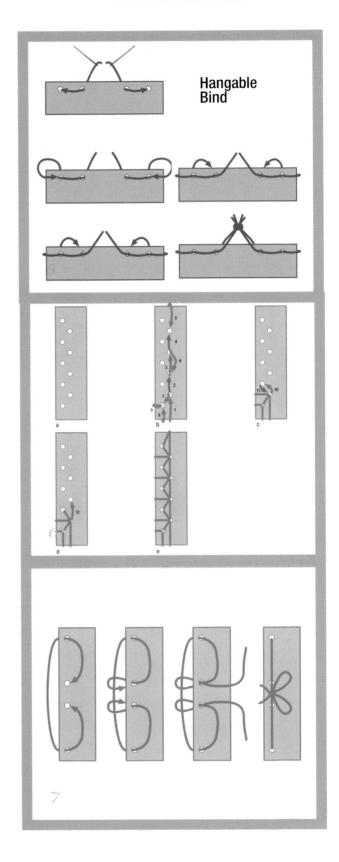

Hangable
Bind

Ideas

• Tie the holes in pairs with leather lacing.

• Use nuts, bolts, and washers to bind the book. Cut off any excess of length on the bolt before assembling.

• Use four-hole buttons attached with cord.

• Use raffia or craft ribbon as a binding.

• Use beads as binding. See Lina Atlake's unique bead-on-wire binding.

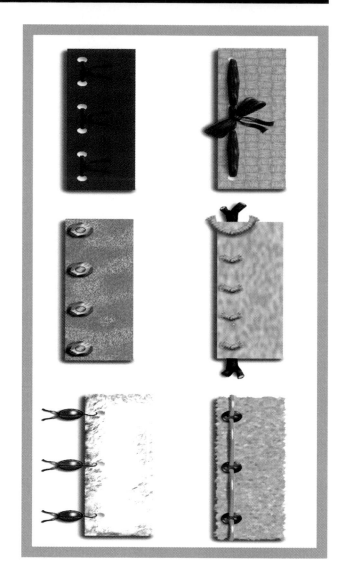

"A tireless scavenger, I collect found objects that contain embedded memories of the past."
——Barbara Seidel

Templates

Scan any of the following templates into your computer and print out as many as you like for your book. You may also take these to a printer and run them off on a copier. Assemble the pages into a glorious bound book.

Anniversary Salute

Guest   Salutations

_____   _____
_____   _____
_____   _____
_____   _____
_____   _____
_____   _____
_____   _____
_____   _____
_____   _____
_____   _____
_____   _____
_____   _____
_____   _____
_____   _____
_____   _____
_____   _____
_____   _____
_____   _____
_____   _____
_____   _____
_____   _____
_____   _____

Birder's Journal

Today's Date_____

Bird_____

Location_____

Comments_____

_____

_____

_____

_____

_____

_____

_____

_____

_____

_____

_____

_____

_____

_____

_____

_____

_____

_____

_____

_____

_____

_____

_____

Use the additional space to record future sightings, note any unusual occurrences, or personal observations. Date each successive entry.

BIRTHDAY BASH

Garden Journal

Date: _____

Common Plant Name: _____

Botanical Name: _____

Where Acquired: _____

_____

Height _____   ○ Perennial   Bloom Time _____   Flower Color _____
                ○ Annual
                ○ Biennial

Where Planted _____

_____

_____

Additional Comments

Moist/Dry   S/PS/Shade

needs acid soil
performs best, size of flower
date all additional entries

Guest Book
PLEASE SIGN IN

Guest Name and Address   Salutations

Personal Journal

Today's Date_____

★ _____

_____

_____

_____

_____

_____

_____

_____

_____

_____

_____

_____

_____

_____

_____

_____

_____

_____

_____

_____

_____

_____

_____

_____

_____

_____

Travel Log

Day _____

Destination _____

Itinerary _____

_____

_____

_____

_____

_____

_____

_____

_____

_____

_____

_____

_____

_____

_____

_____

use empty
space for photo,
sketch, or collage

"Portfolio #8" by Linda Fry Kenzle Portfolio of Japanese paper cardboard construction with acrylic painting, velcro closure

ELEGANT PORTFOLIO

The portfolio makes a nice presentation piece. Fill it with loose sheets of paper, watercolor drawings, charcoal sketches or just penned poems. Remove the flap and finish it off as a slipcase for a bound book. Choose a distinct paper for covering the outside.

MATERIALS

Cardboard (cardboard box weight)	Metal yardstick
1 large sheet decorative paper (lightweight, yet opaque)	Pencil
	Adhesive
1 large sheet liner paper (linen, vellum, etc.)	An old flat paintbrush at least 1" wide for spreading adhesive
Utility knife or rotary cutter	Acrylic paint (optional)

"Books... become a way to integrate both my love of nature and my love for the discovery of creation into one object."

——Julie E. Harris

CONSTRUCTION

1. Measure and cut a piece of cardboard following the diagram.

2. As illustrated, score the cardboard by cutting only partially through the cardboard. This partial cut allows the cardboard to be folded on a precise line. If you have never scored, you may wish to practice scoring on an extra piece of cardboard before doing it on the portfolio piece. Try not to cut deeper than halfway through the cardboard as the score will weaken and can cause tearing.

3. Cover your work surface with waxed paper or plastic wrap. Spread the adhesive onto one side of the cardboard. Lay the cardboard, glue side down, onto the sheet of decorative paper. Let glue dry thoroughly.

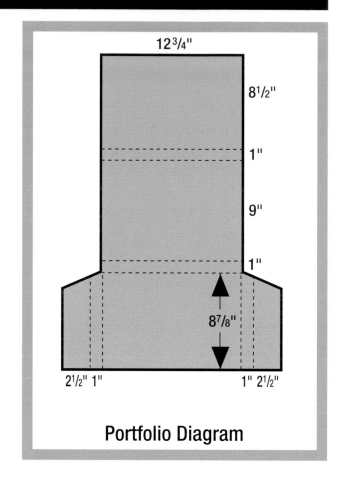

Portfolio Diagram

4. Cut the decorative paper around the cardboard adding a 1" margin for folding.

5. To facilitate turning, make cuts on all inside and outside corners.

6. Fold the decorative paper onto the raw cardboard and glue in place.

7. Lay the portfolio piece on the liner paper and trace. Cut out the liner paper 1/4" inside the tracing line.

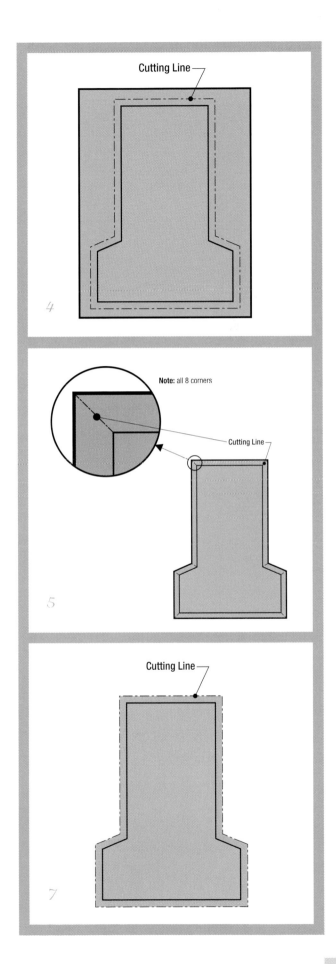

8. Glue the liner to the cardboard. Let dry thoroughly.

9. To construct the portfolio, fold the side flaps to the inside. Fold the bottom flap up and the top flap down. It should now be clear how the portfolio goes together. Open up the portfolio and glue the side flaps in place.

10. Glue the Velcro closure in place.

11. Add additional embellishments. The portfolio shown has applied acrylic paint.

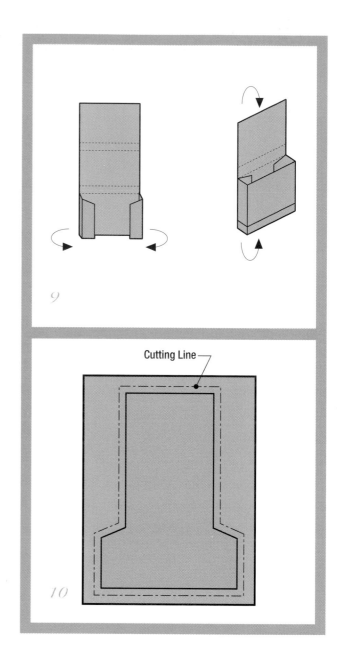

Cutting Line

Considerations

Choose softer, thinner papers for this project. Heavier papers will not have the pliability to cover the cardboard with grace.

I use Tacky™ white glue (PVA) for this project. You may prefer to try a favorite paste recipe.

The scored sections, 1" in this case, determine the width of the finished portfolio. If you wish to create a wider portfolio, enlarge this measurement to the desired size. The portfolio will only fold correctly if both scored sections and the side flap scores are the same measurements.

Make the portfolio in any dimensions. The design shown is perfect to accept 8 1/2" x 11" sheets of paper. Create huge or tiny portfolios to accommodate the pages you wish to insert. Remember to leave extra space so it won't be necessary to squeeze the pages into the portfolio.

Decorate the cover paper before construction.

Ideas

• Make the portfolio tote-able by gluing on leather or webbing straps.

• Try using cloth such as batik, dyed cotton, linen or ultra-leather for covering the portfolio.

• Cut windows in the portfolio flap.

• See my earlier book Embellishments (Chilton, a division of Krause Publications 1993) for elegant knotted closure instructions.

• To create a romantic Victorian style closure, add ribbons between the edge of the decorative paper and the liner.

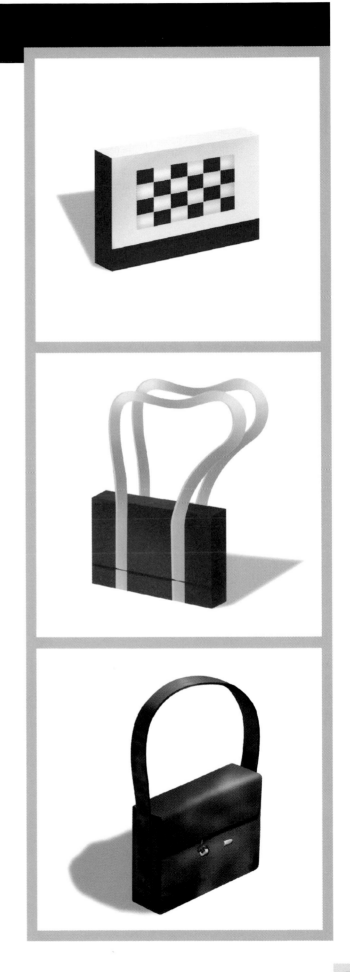

"Cowgirl Love" by Linda Fry Kenzle Album of precut mats, ink drawing on leather binding

THE TREASURED PHOTO ALBUM

Create a unique photo album by using precut picture mats or cutting one from matboard. The featured album contains only five pages to commemorate a Wyoming vacation. Mount the photos on onion skin using photo corners. This type of album is far superior to the store-bought type with acetate pages that, over time, will discolor the photographs. Create a batch of these albums to hold treasured photos.

MATERIALS

Matboard, acid free (or 8 precut matboards 8" x 10")
Onion skin paper - 5 sheets
Utility knife or rotary cutter
Ruler
Pencil
Linen cloth tape
Strip of soft kid leather, 6" x 9" or other material to cover hinge seam
Adhesive

Instructions are given for pictured photo album. However, if desired, create different sizes.

CONSTRUCTION

1. Cut five mats with an outside measurement of 8" x 10" and a window of 5" x 7".

2. Cut five pieces of matboard 1 1/2" x 8" for the flat spine of the album.

1

3. Cut the five sheets of onion skin paper to 6" x 8". Glue a sheet of onion skin paper to the backside of each mat, covering the window opening.

Attach the onion skin paper on the top edge only so it can be lifted to insert the photo. Let the mats dry thoroughly.

4. On the backside, leave a 3/4" gap and tape together a flat spine piece and one of the mats. Be sure to keep everything in alignment. Repeat for the four other flat spines and mats.

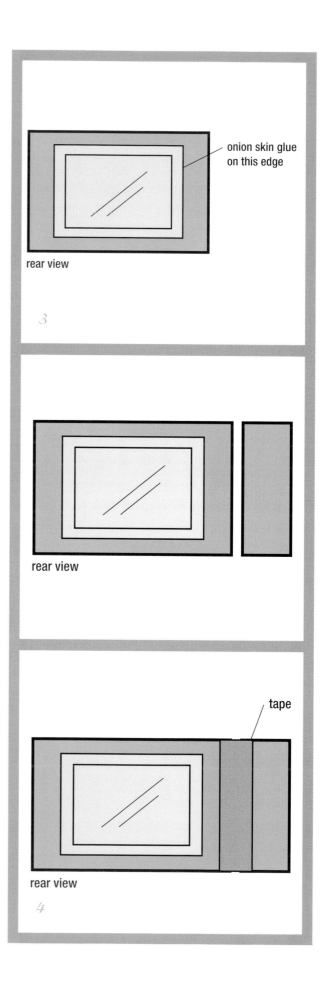

onion skin glue on this edge

rear view

3

rear view

tape

rear view

4

5. Cut a leather strip 2" x 9". To cover the 3/4" gap, glue the strip onto the front of one of the mat/flat spine constructions. Glue the ends of the leather around to the backside of the mat.

6. In a stacking fashion, glue together the flat spine sections of each of the mats. The leather piece should be on top. Let dry.

7. Cut a 9" x 11 3/4" piece of matboard to create the back board. Keeping the pages in alignment, glue the last flat spine section to this backing board.

8. At this point, add additional embellishments such as extra leather adornment or drawings.

9. Use photo corners to mount the photographs on the onion skin paper. If desired, seal the onion skin with adhesive.

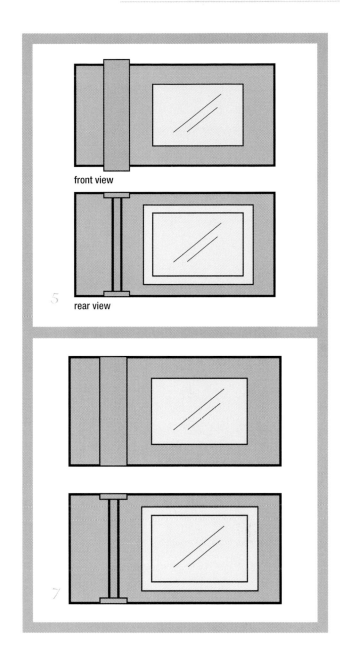

front view

5   rear view

7

Considerations

If cutting mats, coordinate the size of the window opening with the size of your photographs.

In place of onion skin, consider using any thin decorative paper such as rice paper.

To cover the hinge, use any non-fraying fabric such as felt or ultraleather.

Ideas

Cut the mats in shapes to correspond with the theme of the album. For example, use the shape of an old-fashioned school house for an album memorializing school days.

Create an elegant version in linen with satin rattail cord for binding.

Use window cut-outs in any desired shape.

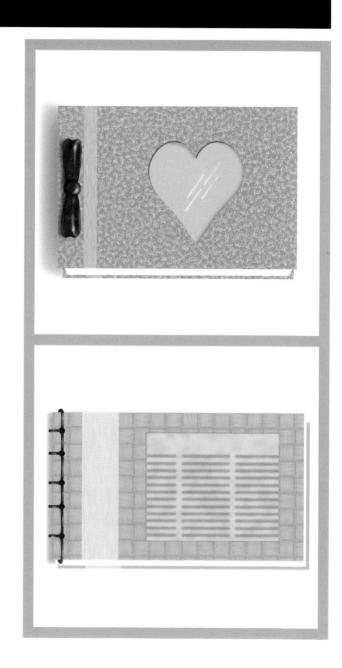

How about a Plexiglas cover with huge binding rings?

Work out a design using loop hinges.

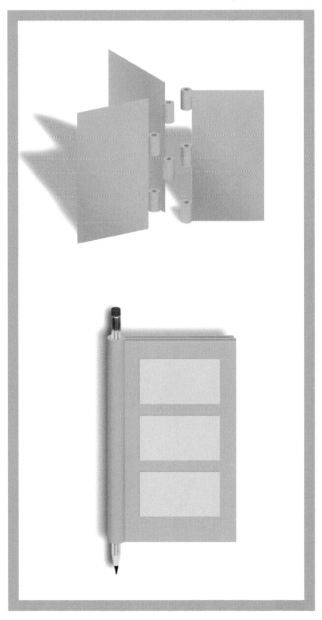

PART FOUR
Design Potentials

Mold and deckle with handmade paper samples

HANDMADE PAPER

Handmade paper is made quite easily. Any fibers, such as torn bits of natural cloth including wool, silk or cotton, strips of paper, dryer lint, snippets of threads in both metallic and regular, and even dried flower petals, can be compressed together to create a sheet of handmade paper. The resulting paper is textural and beautiful, quite unlike the heavily-compressed sheets of paper available at the local school supply store.

To create your own paper you will need a few supplies: See the **Resource** *list for information on purchasing and entire papermaking kit for $20 to $30. All materials listed below are included.*

Deckle and mold - The deckle is an open frame used to create a form for the handmade paper. The mold is a frame with a screen attached to the opening. They are sold as a set and are readily available from suppliers.

Plastic tub - Large enough to fit the mold and deckle.

Blender - Needed to create the paper pulp.

Felts - Pieces of cloth or heavy paper, cut to the size of the mold for compressing the paper.

Sponge - Needed to absorb excess water from the paper.

Papermaking fibers - Watercolor paper, cotton batting, dryer lint, flowers, etc.

Essential oil - Optional.

PAPERMAKING

1. Add 3 cups of water to the blender. Tear 1/2 of a 5" x 7" sheet of watercolor paper into small pieces about the size of an Oreo™ cookie and add to blender. Let the paper soak in the water while you assemble the rest of the materials.

2. Include dryer lint and puffs of cotton batting to add a bit of fiber and color. Carefully choose a color for the final paper. Being careful not to overblend, mix until the fibers form cloud-like shapes and appear watery. Be sure there are no large lumps.

3. Add any additional materials such as bits of gold thread, dried flower petals, crushed dried vegetable leaves. Essential oils may also be added to scent the paper and act as a preservative/insect repellent. Blend.

4. Place the mold and deckle in the plastic tub. Fill the tub with water to cover.

5. Optional - If you wish to size the paper to hold inks and paints, add two tablespoon of liquid starch to the tub of water. Stir in thoroughly.

6. Pour the contents of the blender into the tub and stir.

7. Immediately insert the mold and deckle vertically, screen side up, so the pulp is above the frame. Pull the frame straight up. Lock the fibers together by quickly shaking the frame from side-to-side to create an even distribution of the pulp. The pulp should evenly cover the screen.

8. Use the sponge to absorb the water. Wring sponge and continue soaking up water until no more is absorbed.

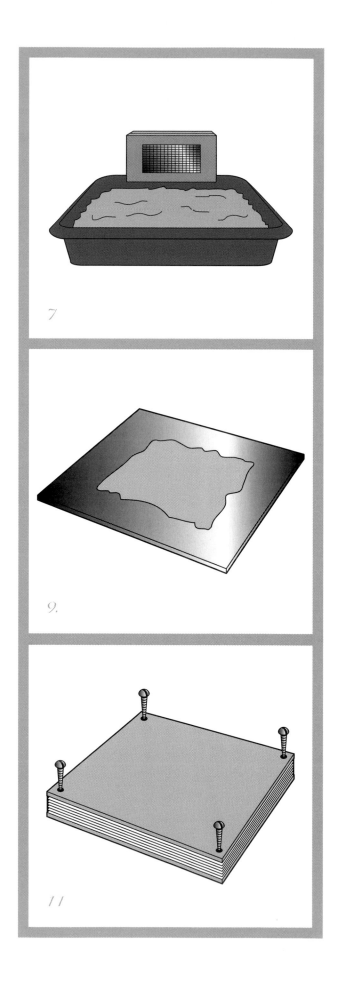

9. Place one of the felts on the pulp and gently press out any water. Carefully knock out the piece of paper, from the back of the mold, onto a stack of newspaper. Remove the felt. Let paper dry.

10. Continue making sheets of paper with the rest of the pulp.

11. On a hot , dry day place the sheets of paper, with felts interspaced, between two pieces of wood. Clamp together on each of the four corners to make certain that the paper dries evenly and does not take on a wavy appearance.

This creates a cold-pressed paper. For a hot-press paper, iron the paper. For a rough finish, simply air-dry the paper.

12. When the paper has little or no moisture, store it in a dry spot to prevent further absorption of water from the atmosphere.

TROUBLESHOOTING

• If the pieces of paper or cloth remain whole, soak for a longer time.

• If more color is desired, add more lint or brightly colored tissue paper to create a new color.

• First timers usually insert the deckle and mold upside down. Be sure the screen is toward the top.

• If the pulp does not cover adequately, reinsert the mold and deckle into the tub, or spoon a bit of pulp into the weak areas.

• If the dried paper creates troughs of applied ink or paint, add more size to the next batch. Reserve these paper for collage work or other projects where you will not be making direct applications.

• If paper has dried crinkled, spritz it on both sides with plain water and place it between two boards as instructed in step number 11.

• Do not pour excess pulp down the drain as it will create a clog. Drain the pulp out of the water and discard in the garbage. The tub of pulp and water can also be thrown on your compost pile.

• To create sculptural pieces, lay the piece of damp paper over a form and allow to dry.

After successfully creating sheets of paper, try adding glitter, confetti, onion skins, crepe paper, old envelopes and correspondence, gift wrap, typing paper, computer paper, minced celery, asparagus, beets, tissue paper, thin leaves, coffee, tea, decorative yarns, seed beads, food coloring, silk dyes or spices such as turmeric and cinnamon. You can even add pet hair!

Any thick materials should be boiled, to break down the fibers, before they are added to the pulp mixture. At the least, soak the fibers overnight. Experiment.

"The current generation of artists makes use of some of the basic structures of the codex and flies off into the blue for the finish." ——Pat Baldwin

EMBOSSING

"Bubble Wrap" (in progress) by Linda Fry Kenzle Handmade paper molded on a rubber stamp

Add subtle textural effects to the handmade paper by trying this easy embossing technique.

For a tone-on-tone effect, press objects into the paper before the paper is completely dry. If paper is already dry, spritz with water, on both sides, to gently soften. Some of the areas will be compressed flat while others will remain raised. Try using a lace doily, rubber stamps, pressed leaves, nuts and bolts, a wire design, seed beads, cookie molds, fancy ice cube trays, or any other object that will make an interesting design.

Place the object on the damp paper and weight it down with a piece of wood and clamps or a stack of books. When the paper is slightly damp, remove the weights and allow the piece to dry completely.

PART FIVE

Paper Enhancement Methods

STAMPING

Rubber stamps are available in a vast array of images. If preferable, take a simple drawing to a copy center and have the image made into a one-of-a-kind rubber stamp. Stamps can also be cut from erasers with an Exacto™ knife, leaving a reverse image.

Stamped samples using hand-cut eraser stamps on various printing papers

Printing the stamps on paper requires ink or paint and an applicator or ink pad. Paper towels are also necessary to wipe a previous color off of a stamp and keep your hands and work space clean.

I like fabric paints and acrylics because they can be applied to the stamp with a paintbrush or a foam brush. Create your own ink pad by using layers of folded felt, or if preferable, purchase an un-inked pad. Saturate the pad with dye or ink and its ready to use. Inks and dyes used for silk painting give intense transparent colors.

Apply the color to the stamp. Check the print of the image, before actually printing on your handmade paper. Stamp the image on the newspaper or a scrap of the finished paper.

Consider cutting a signature or monogram stamp, also called a chop, and use it to mark your books. See the right-hand corner of the fishing scroll on page 36.

Try printing the stamp by creating special effects:
Twist the image as you print.
Make layered images.
Create multiple images without re-inking.
Form images into shapes, such as a mandala.
Ink different sections of the stamp in various
     colors.
Combine stamps and drawings or watercolors.

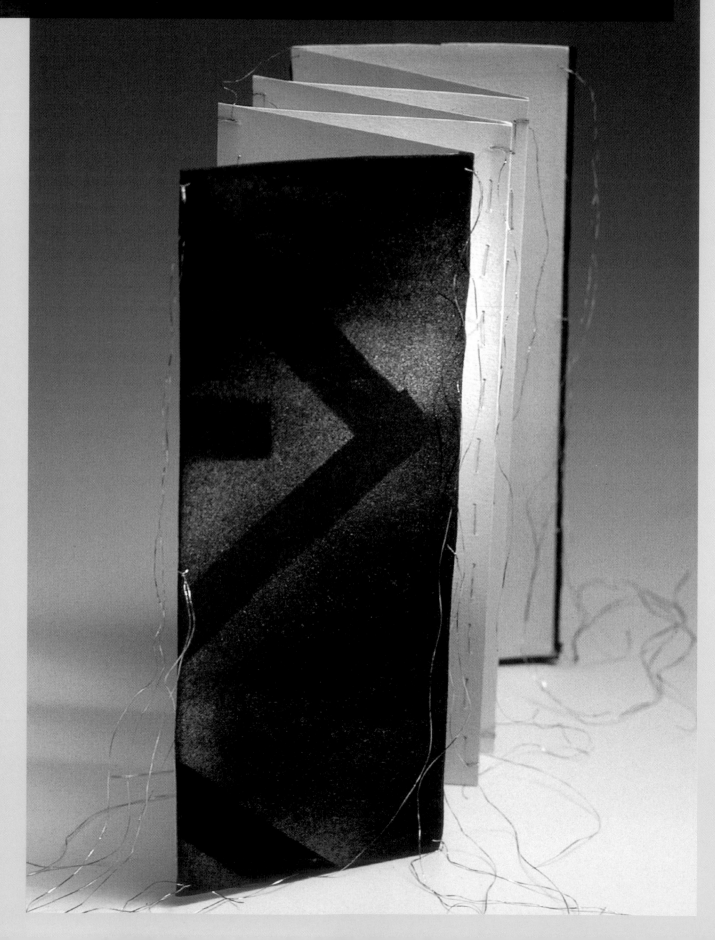

STENCILING

An intriguing way to create images on paper is with the use of stencils or masks. Here an opening is cut into a piece of heavy paper, special stencil plastic or mylar. The positive images are then printed onto the book paper.

Although there are many commercial stencils available, I prefer to cut personal images for stenciling. Cutting a stencil requires an Exacto™ knife and one of the stencil materials mentioned above. Transfer design to stencil material and cut out the image.

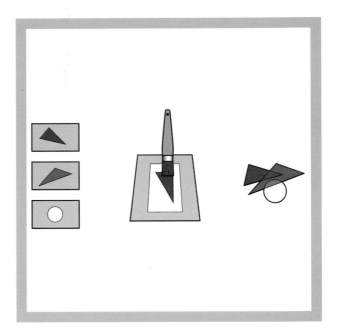

Stenciling can also be done by using masks, such as masking tape friskets, or any object that will block out the paint, creating negative images.

Place acrylic paint on a palette or dish and insert a special flat-topped stencil brush in the paint. Dab off a bit of the paint onto a stack of newspaper. Stencil the image. Avoid building up a rim of paint on the edge of the stencil. Use a soft sweeping motion and build up the paint in layers to intensify the final image.

Again, try some special effects:
Overlapping.
Stenciling one sharp image and many
    soft-edged images.
Use the same stencil with many different
    colors of paint.
Try wax resists as a way to mask out areas. Rub
    a candle over a sheet of paper that has
    been lain on a textured surface, such as
    corrugated cardboard. Paint. When dry,
    remove the wax with a hot iron.

Left: "Alchemist's Blackboard" by Linda Fry Kenzle Accordion book with cloth covers masked and sprayed with gold fabric paint, gold lame' thread

SPRAYING

"Sky Chunk" by Linda Fry Kenzle Ribbon bound book of watercolor paper sprayed and collaged with glassine piece

Create an all-over pattern by using spattering. Dip a toothbrush into paint or dye and, while directing the spatters onto the paper, rub a credit card across it.

Or, dilute paint, place it in a fine-spray bottle and spritz the paper.

To create special effects:
• Spray the paper and pick it up immediately to create streaks of paint.
• Spray into a stencil opening.
• Create a pointillist effect by using colors next to each other. This visually creates other colors. For instance, spray blue in one section and abut it with yellow spray. The final effect in the center, where the colors meet, will appear green. Note the color wheel on page 95 for additional color combinations.

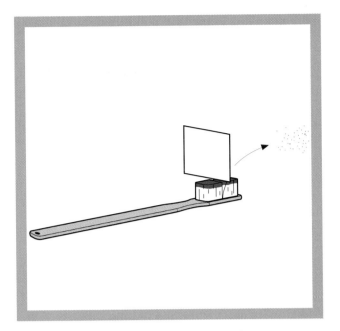

"I selected the accordian format as the structural form to emphasize the concept of the unfolding of time or the facets of change."
——Katherine Venturelli

"TransFormation" by Linda Fry Kenzle Scroll of handmade paper, dowels, collage, stitching

If a sewing machine is available, don't overlook the possibilities of this tool. Thread the machine and insert the paper under the presser foot. Start sewing to discover what effects can be created. To work a more artful design, release the feed dogs and move the paper with your hands. Control the speed and direction using a free hand motion. Experiment with decorative threads or couch over thick threads, in a zigzag stitch, with regular thread.

If a sewing machine is not available, use a large needle, decorative threads and cords to create an exotic surface decoration.

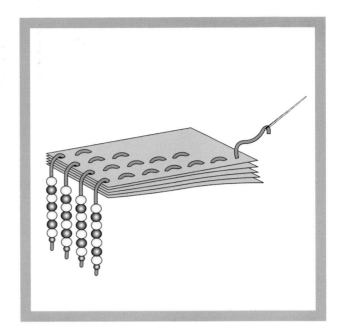

Thread ends can be knotted or left to hang loose. If the threads are not structural, anything goes!

Once you have approached sewing as an idea for ornamenting your paper, you can use stitches to affix items onto the paper. Add cloth, emblems, charms or sticks. Any interesting item you envision will bring intrigue to the final piece.

"The human story reveals itself through a vast library of books and booklike structures."

——Miriam Schaer

MARBLING

"Loud Whispers" by Linda Fry Kenzle Accordion book with marbled silk covers

Long ago, books and the art of marbling made a marriage. Perhaps your first exposure to marbling was the swirled-design **end papers** of an old leather bound book. End papers are on the inside of the front and back covers. There are two ways to achieve beautiful marbling. The first uses an oil and water method, the second employs the newer paint formulations. Both methods produce outstanding results with little experience in the techniques. The number of colors and the hues of the colors you use can yield subtle or bold effects. Any design can be attained, from sophisticated statements to playful, even funky moods.

Method One

This method is based on the concept that oil and water don't mix. Essentially, oil paint is floated on water, then transferred to paper.

To begin the following materials are required:
- Oil paint.
- Turpentine.
- A large cookie sheet or butcher's tray.
- Paper or cloth, *see below.*
- Manipulators such as pencils, sticks and large-toothed combs with some of the teeth removed .

A large plastic garbage bag.
Old newspapers.

1. Fill the pan or tray with water.
2. Add turpentine to oil paints to create a thick consistency that will still easily pour.
3. Pour the paint onto the surface of the water. Use various colors in different areas. Draw through the paint using some of the manipulators. Stop when an attractive pattern is achieved.
4. To print, carefully lay a sheet of paper onto the water surface and immediately remove. To dry, place the paper right side up on a plastic garbage bag.

4

5. To continue marbling, first remove the paint by placing 3" strips of newspaper on the water surface. Gently and immediately remove the newspaper strips. The newspaper will pick up the paint. Continue using sheets of newspaper until the water surface is clear. Once again add paint, manipulate, and print.

Marbling Two

This method uses water-soluble paint. A suspension medium is required to hold the paint on the surface for printing. I have used three different media: carageenan, Irish Moss, liquid starch, and wallpaper paste. Try any of the four and discover their effects.

You'll need:
- Any acrylic-based paint. Fabric paints gave a nice flow.
- A wide, shallow container.
- A suspension medium.
- Paper or cloth, *see below.*
- Manipulators such as combs or sticks.
- A large plastic garbage bag.

1. Set up the suspension medium. Choose one:

    a. The liquid starch is used straight from the bottle.

    b. Prepare the wallpaper paste as directed on the package.

    c. Prepare the carageenan by mixing 2 tablespoons of the powder in 1 gallon of warm water. Place the mixture in a blender or beat with a wire whisk. Dissolve as much of the powder as possible. It is acceptable if all of the mixture does not dissolve. Pour the suspension liquid into a shallow 13" x 15" pan. The liquid gel will be approxi mately 11/4" deep. Let the carageenan sit overnight or a minimum of 12 hours. Remove air bubbles that have formed on the surface.

d. Prepare Irish moss by filling a roasting pan with water. Cover the waters surface by sprinkling with Irish moss. Bring the water to a boil. Allow to cool and congeal overnight.

2. Drop paint onto the surface and manipulate into attractive patterns. Avoid overworking colors or they will become muddy and drop to the bottom of the suspension gel.

3. Carefully lay a sheet of paper on the surface. Pull it up and off, then lay it to dry right side up on a plastic garbage bag. Don't try to hold the paper perpendicular or the colors will run, thus ruining the design. Do not use until the paper is completely dry.

A WORD ON COLOR

It is helpful to have some knowledge of color mixing when using the marbling methods. Primary colors are red, yellow, and blue. Secondary colors are orange - a mixture of red and yellow; green - a mixture of yellow and blue; and purple - a mixture of red and blue; each mixed in equal amounts. Tertiaries are unequal amounts of two primaries. For example, red orange is a mixture of a large amount of red with a dash of yellow. Color change is the magical aspect of marbling.

TROUBLE SHOOTING

- Slick paper will not work with marbling, try a felted or cold-pressed watercolor paper.
- If you produce a pattern with an area that did not marble, an air bubble may have been trapped between the paper and the water surface. Lay the paper on the water surface, rather than dropping it in place.
- The marbling has been overworked if the design appears indistinct. Avoid breaking down the paint, before marbling, by planning the design before manipulating.
- If you get odd "eye" patterns in the centers of a stone pattern, pick them up with a small piece of newspaper before printing.
- If the paint does not adhere to the paper, use a mordant as you would for cloth. Instructions follow:

MARBLING CLOTH

If using a marbling technique on cloth rather than paper, you will need to first mordant the cloth. A mordant serves to adhere paint to the cloth. Mordanting also can be used to create papers that accept the paint more readily.

To mordant the cloth, prepare it by soaking in tepid water, then wring out the cloth. In a plastic dishpan, add 3 tablespoons alum for each quart of warm water. Stirring occasionally, soak the damp cloth in the alum/water mixture for one hour. Alum is available in the herb and spice section of the supermarket.

Remove the cloth, wring it out, and hang to dry. Do not rinse the mordant from the cloth. It will be removed after the marbling process. Proceed with the marbling technique described above.

Color Wheel

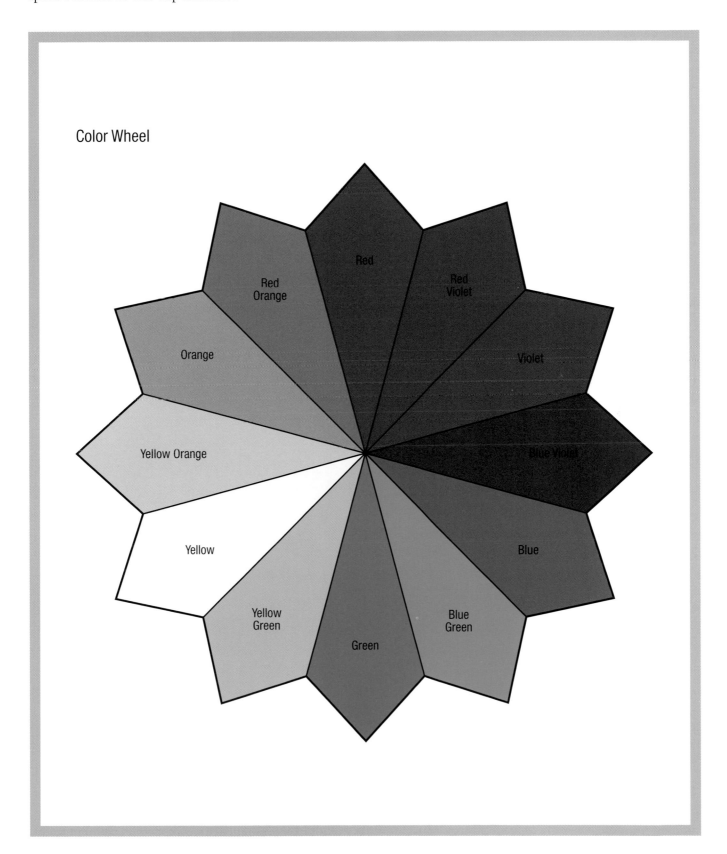

CUTTING

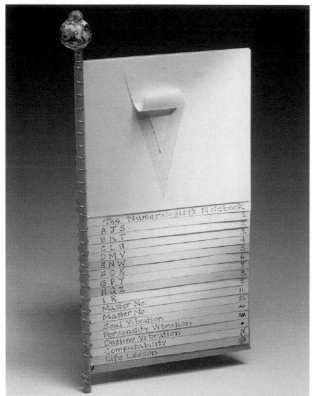

"Numerologist's Notebook" by Linda Fry Kenzle

Change the paper's surface provocatively by cutting into it whereby disrupting the serene quality of a pristine sheet of paper.

Make cuts in paper by using an Exacto™, single-edged razor blade or knife. To create a rhythm, repeat the exact same cut across the papers surface. Evoke a prickly surface by cutting sharp pointed cuts into paper. Or, create a soft serene feeling with a rounded cut.

Take cutting a step further into weaving. Cut two sheets of paper into strips. Recreate them into a woven sheet of paper by weaving the strips in an under/over tabby weave.

Because cutting is often interesting and sophisticated, it begs further exploration. Consider tearing the paper into patterns rather then cutting it with a sharp instrument.

I'm confident that you will invent other creative ways to sculpture the paper.

Build up the papers surface with collage by using your newly acquired skills of embossing, stamping, stenciling, spraying, sewing, marbling, and cutting.

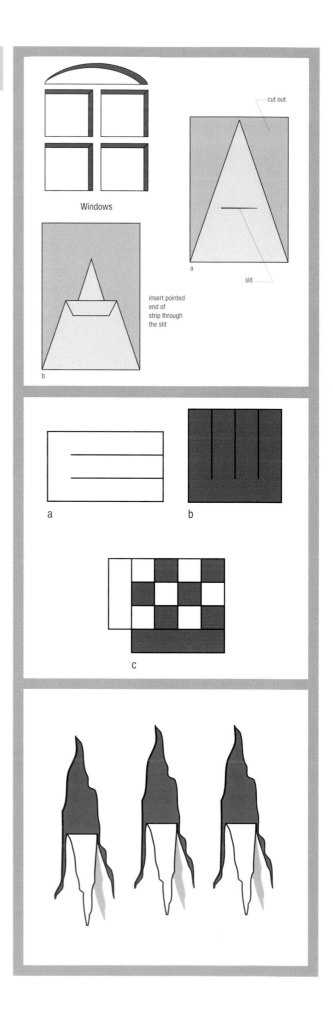

COLLAGE

"During" by Linda Fry Kenzle Accordion book of water-color wash and salt technique, gold leaf

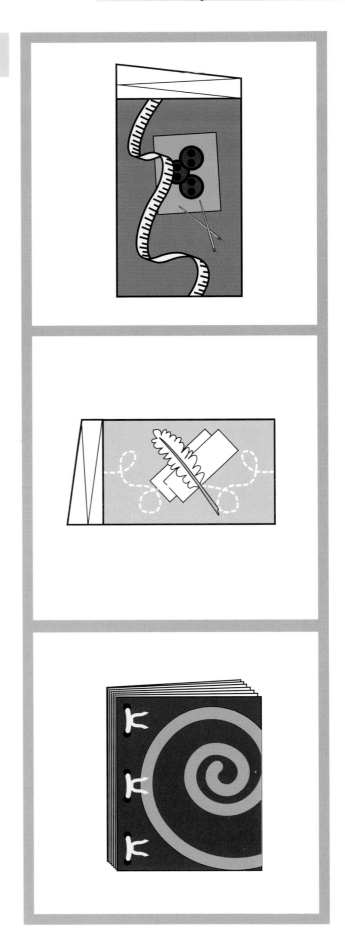

To collage, select materials to layer upon the papers surface. While selecting different elements, consider line, form, space, texture, proportion, and color. Work with whatever comes your way; paper cut-outs, mylar, aluminum sheets, metal, buttons, feathers, gold leaf, found objects. Experiment. Work spontaneously. Let the design emerge. Stop when your eye and heart are satisfied.

ET CETERA

There are many ways to infuse your spirit into books.

Here are a few ideas:
Blueprinting
Dyeing
Batik
Printmaking Techniques such as woodcuts, wood engraving, etching, resist patterns, lithographs, serigraphs, and aquatints.
Cloth Techniques like quilting, tucking, pleating, smocking, and other manipulations.
Air Brush
Beading
Gocco Printing
Laminating, Rubbings
Watercolor Techniques such as wet-into-wet, salt techniques, and paint scraping.
Nature Printing
Castings
Pop-Ups
Calligraphy
Xerox Transfers

Try mixing media. Allow the first medium to dry before applying a second medium. Don't apply water-based media over oils or the surface will crack off.

The bibliography lists some books that cover these techniques. Consider the bibliography a road map to a great adventure. Materialize your creative dreams.

"The book form is familiar to everyone and infinitely variable."

——Mary Tyler

PART SIX
Artist's Showcase

Magritte's studio contained two buckets...

...rrying and we conten...

...he was here or...

there

MINI MAGRITTE
Magritte's Buckets

Magritte's
Buckets
Charles Hobson

Magritte's studio contained two buck-
ets. One day he tried to measure the height of the tides using the two buckets, one filled with clouds and one filled with rain, but

"Magritte's Buckets" by Charles Hobson Sculptural book with two monotypes

"Ars Poetica" by Beverly Nichols

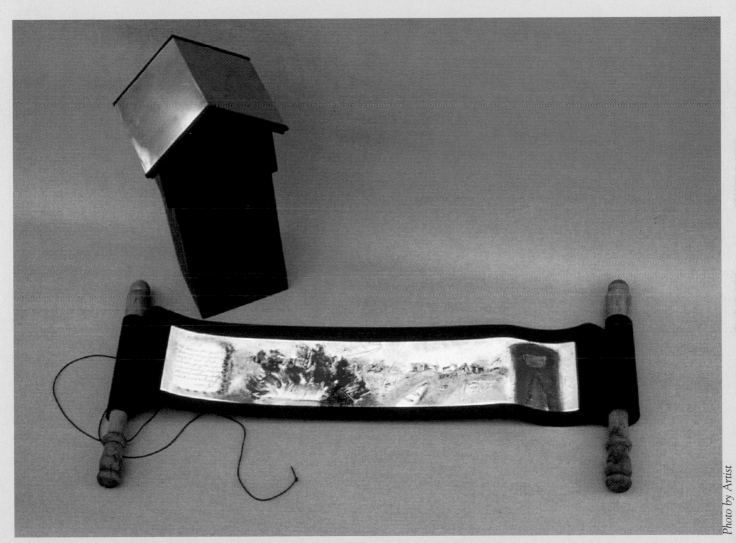

"Prophecy Series-Scroll One by Katherine Venturelli Monotype with copper leaf encased in wood/copper

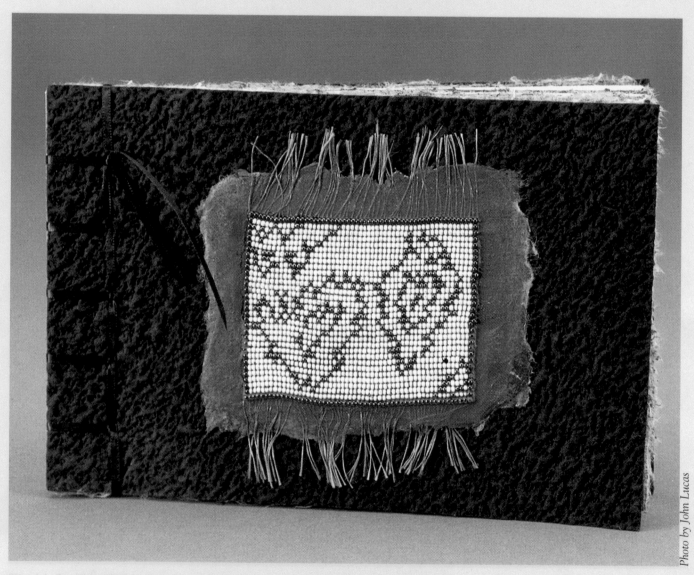

Wendy's Book" by Gail Looper Japanese bound book with beaded loomwork set in handmade paper cover, Indian coral reef paper cover

"Mountain I" by Mary Ellen Long Buried paper, sand, rock, stamped text

"Fish Book I" by Mary Tyler Folded spring bound book, photocopy transfers, paste papers

"Fruity Jubilee" by Pat Baldwin

" *Spirit Book #8:Earth Rood*" *by Susan Kapuscinski Gaylord Handmade Mexican bark paper, Japanese kyo paper, binder boards, brass, wooden, and glass beads, jute, twigs, and thread on a honeysuckle branch*

"Letters of Obsession" by Susan Hensel Handmade paper, faux postage, and text by the artist , produced on a Macintosh computer

"Chameleons on Parade" by Anne-Claude Cotty Collaged paste papers, shaped accordion sewn into a 2-sided cloth case

Photo by Darwin Davidson

"My Wish" by Karen Page Three-dimensional book

the grove

*"The Grove" by Barbara
Seidel Mixed media book*

"No More Dishes to Wash" by Miriam Schaer Doll house dishes, metal toy sink, Xerox, acrylic, and ink

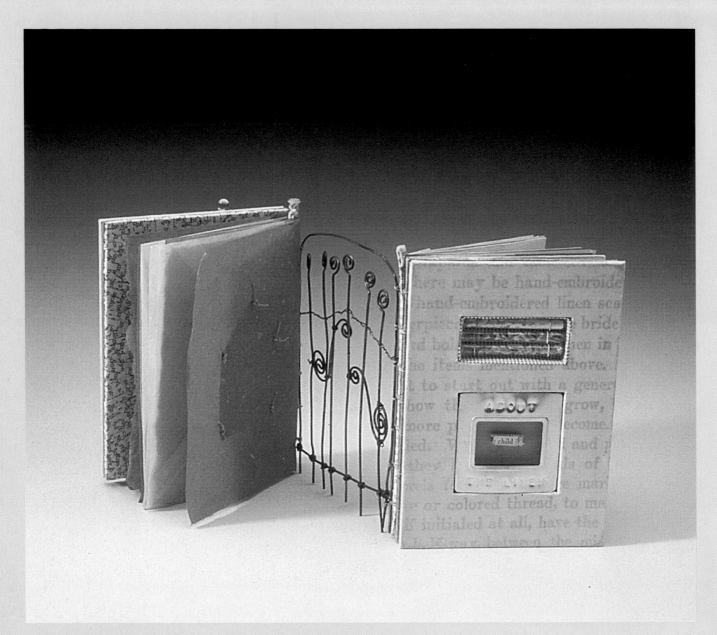

"About the Linens" by Joan Soppe Letterpress, mixed media and handmade paper

PART SEVEN
The Last Word

PRESERVATION

Take care in preserving your beautiful books, scrolls, journals, and albums. Ideally, paper should be stored flat in a cool, dark room with 45% to 70% humidity. Fluctuations in temperature, such as an attic without insulation, can destroy paper. Moisture in a basement will create a haven for mold. Bright light will fade the paper and activate the aging process. Even acid-free, archival materials will be destroyed under adverse conditions.

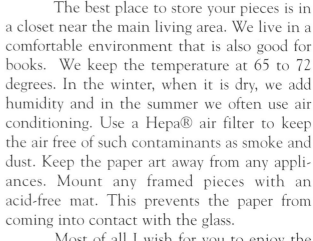

The best place to store your pieces is in a closet near the main living area. We live in a comfortable environment that is also good for books. We keep the temperature at 65 to 72 degrees. In the winter, when it is dry, we add humidity and in the summer we often use air conditioning. Use a Hepa® air filter to keep the air free of such contaminants as smoke and dust. Keep the paper art away from any appliances. Mount any framed pieces with an acid-free mat. This prevents the paper from coming into contact with the glass.

Most of all I wish for you to enjoy the pieces you've created. Write in your journals and display your art pieces. Later, when you store these treasures, take care to preserve them for the pleasure of future generations.

...while you are offered many dizzying opportunities in a lifetime, Spirit only comes once for each Work seeking creative expression through you, then moves on. The bottom line is that the Work must be brought forth. If you don't do it, someone else will. So when that great idea flashes across your mind surrounded by Light, pay attention!

Once it exists in your mind, realize that other brainwaves soon will be able to pick up the creative energy pattern if they are receptive. Think of your mind as a satellite dish. Creative celestial images are continuously being transmitted. The frequency is jammed-privy to your soul only- for an infinitesimal, proprietary moment. Just long enough for you to lift up your heart, accept the assignment, and give thanks.

-Sarah Ban Breathnach

INDEX

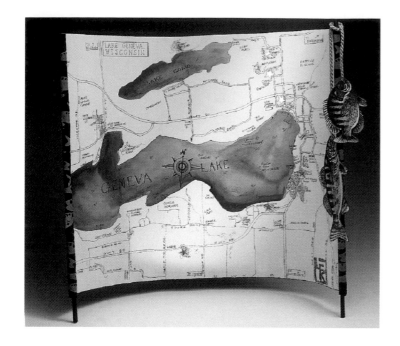

BIBLIOGRAPHY

Banister, Manly *The Craft of Bookbinding,* Dover, New York, 1975

Barker, Vicki, and Tesesa Bird *The Art of Quilting* E.P.Dutton, New York, 1988

Bethmann, Laura Donnelly *Nature Printing* Storey Publishing, 1996

Betti, Claudia and Teel Sale *Drawing Holt,* Rhinehart,and Winston, New York, 1980

Bosence, Susan *Hand Block Printing & Resist Dyeing* David & Charles, London, 1991

Crawford, Maureen *Handmade Greeting Cards* Sterling Publishing, New York, 1992

Edwards, Betty, *Drawing on the Artist Within* Simon & Schuster, New York, 1986

Ekiguchi, Kunio *Gift Wrapping* Kodansha International, Tokyo, 1985

Ferrier, Jean-Louis *Art of the Century* Prentice Hall, New York, 1988

Haysom, Cari *Stampcraft* Chilton Book Co. Radnor, PA 1996

Ikegami, Kojiro *Japanese Bookbinding* Weatherhill, New York, 1979

Irvine, Joan *How to make Pop-ups* Beech Tree Press, New York, 1987

Johnson, Cathy Creative *Textures in Watercolor* North Light Books, Cincinnati, OH 1992

Johnson, Pauline *Creative Bookbinding* Dover, New York, 1963

Justema, William *The Pleasures of Pattern* Reinhold Books, New York, 1968

Kenzle, Linda Fry *Embellishments* Chilton Book Co., Radnor, PA, 1993

Kenzle, Linda Fry *The Irresistible Bead* Chilton Book Co., Radnor, PA, 1996

Kitagawa, Yoshiko *Creative Cards* Kodansha International, Tokyo, 1987

Kondo, Yoko *Creative Gift Packaging* Ondorisha, Tokyo, 1986

LaPlantz, Shereen *Cover to Cover* Lark Books, Asheville, NC, 1995

Laury, Jean Ray *Imagery on Fabric* C&T Publishing, Lafayette, CA 1992

Leland, Nita *The Creative Artist* North Light Books, Cincinnati, Ohio, 1990

Littlejohn, Jean *Fabrics For Embroidery* The Bath Press, London, 1986

Meilach, Donna *Contemporary Batik & Tie-Dye* Crown Books, New York, 1973

Medeiros, Wendy Addison *Marbling Techniques* Watson Guptill, New York, 1994

Morrison, Alex *Photofinish* Van Nostrand-Reinhold, New York, 1981

Moseley, Spenser, and Pauline Johnson, Hazel Koenig *Crafts Design* Wadsworth Publishing, Belmont, CA 1962

Newman, Thelma,et al. *Paper as Art and Craft*, Crown Publishing, New York, 1973

Nice, Claudia *Creating Textures in Pen & Ink with Watercolor* North Light Books, Cincinnati, OH 1995

Peck, Judith *Sculpture as Experience* Chilton Book Co. Radnor, PA 1989

Reep, Edward *The Content of Watercolor* Van Nostrand Reinhold, New York, 1983

Roycraft, Roland *Fill Your Watercolors with Light and Color* North Light Books, Cincinnati, OH 1990

Saddington, Marianne *Making Your Own Paper* Storey Publications, Pownal, VT, 1992

Smith, Keith *Non-Adhesive Binding* Sigma Foundation, Fairport, New York, 1990

Stearns, Lynn (ed.) *Papermaking* Lark Books, Asheville, NC, 1992

Stribling, Mary Lou *Art From Found Materials* Crown Publishing, New York, 1980

Studley, Vance *The Art and Craft of Papermaking* Davis Publications, Worcester, MA 1983

Taylor, Jacqueline *Painting and Embroidery on Silk* Cassell, London, 1992

Toale, Bernard *Basic Printmaking Techniques* Davis Publications, Worcester, MA 1992

Twelvetrees, Kate *Glorious Greetings* Chilton Book Co, Radnor, PA, 1996

Yates Marypaul *Textiles: A Handbook for Designers,* New York, 1986

Wade, Davis *Geometric Patterns & Borders* Van Nostrand Reinhold, New York, 1982

Webberley, Marilyn and JoAn Forsyth *Books, Boxes & Wraps* Bifocal Publishing, Kirkland, WA, 1995

Zeier, Franz Books, *Boxes and Portfolios* Design Press, New York, 1990

RESOURCES

Aiko's Art Materials
3347 North Clark Street
Chicago, IL 06057
773-404-5600
Papers

Amsterdam Art
1013 University Ave.
Berkeley, CA 94710
510-649-4800
General supplies

Art 2 Art
P.O. Box 8370
Springfield, MO 65801
orders: 800-284-8190
General supplies

Artist's Connection
600 U.S. Highway One
Iselin, NJ 08830-2635
order: 800-851-9333
Papers and other supplies

Book Arts Classified
P.O. Box 77167
Washington, DC 20013
please write

Collage
P.O.Box 7216
San Francisco, CA
94120-7216
orders: 800-926-5524
Papermaking kit, finished
books

Colophon Book Arts
3046 Hogun Bay Road
NE
Olympia, WA 98506
360-459-2940
General supplies

Conservation Resources
8000 Forbes Place
Springfield, VA 22151
703-321-7730

Daniel Smith
4128 First St.
Seattle, WA 98134
206-223-9599
orders: 800-426-6740
General supplies

Dick Blick
P.O.Box 1267
Galesburg, IL
61402-1267
309-343-6181
Supplies

Exposures
1 Memory Lane
P.O. Box 3615
Oshkosh, WI 54903
orders: 800-222-4947
Acid-free files and more

Flax Art & Design
1699 Market Street
San Francisco, CA 94107
415-552-2355
General supplies

**Graphic Chemical &
Ink Co.**
728 North Yale Ave.
P.O. Box 27
Villa Park, IL 60181
630-832-6004
Rolls of paper, inks, other
supplies

Ink & Gall
P.O.Box 1469
Taos, NM 87571
Please write
Marbling materials and a
marbling magazine

John Neal Bookseller
1833 Spring Garden St.
Greensboro, NC 27403
910-272-6139
Supplies and books for
the book arts

Light Impressions
P.O. Box 940
Rochester, NY 14607
716-461-4447
Archival supplies

**New York Central
Supply**
62 Third Ave.
New York, NY 10003
212-477-0400
General supplies

**Options! Newsletter
Pardies Inc.**
28 Maya Loop
Santa Fe, NM 87050
Please write

Paper Source
232 West Chicago
Avenue
Chicago, IL 60610
312-337-0798
Papers and supplies

Savoir-Faire
P.O. Box 2021
Sausalito, CA 94966
415-332-4660
Marbling paint

Sax Arts & Crafts
100 East Pleasant Street
Milwaukee, WI 53212
414-784-6880
General supplies

Talas
213 West 35th St.
New York, NY 10001
212-736-7744
Papers and supplies

University Products
P.O.Box 101
Holyoke, MA 01041
413-532-3372
Archival supplies

Linda Fry Kenzle, well-known artist and designer, has work in collections in the United States, Europe, Australia, and Canada. She is the author of nine books. Her next book celebrates another of her passions-creativity in the garden.

Linda lives in the Middle West with her husband, poet Don Carlo. Their son, Joshua, creates welded sculptures.